Meet the Challenge

Problem solving is a survival skill.

SCHOLASTIC

LITERACY PLACE ®

Copyright acknowledgments and credits appear on page 144, which constitutes an extension of this copyright page.

2 3 4 5 6 7 8 9 10   24   02 01 00 99 98 97 96

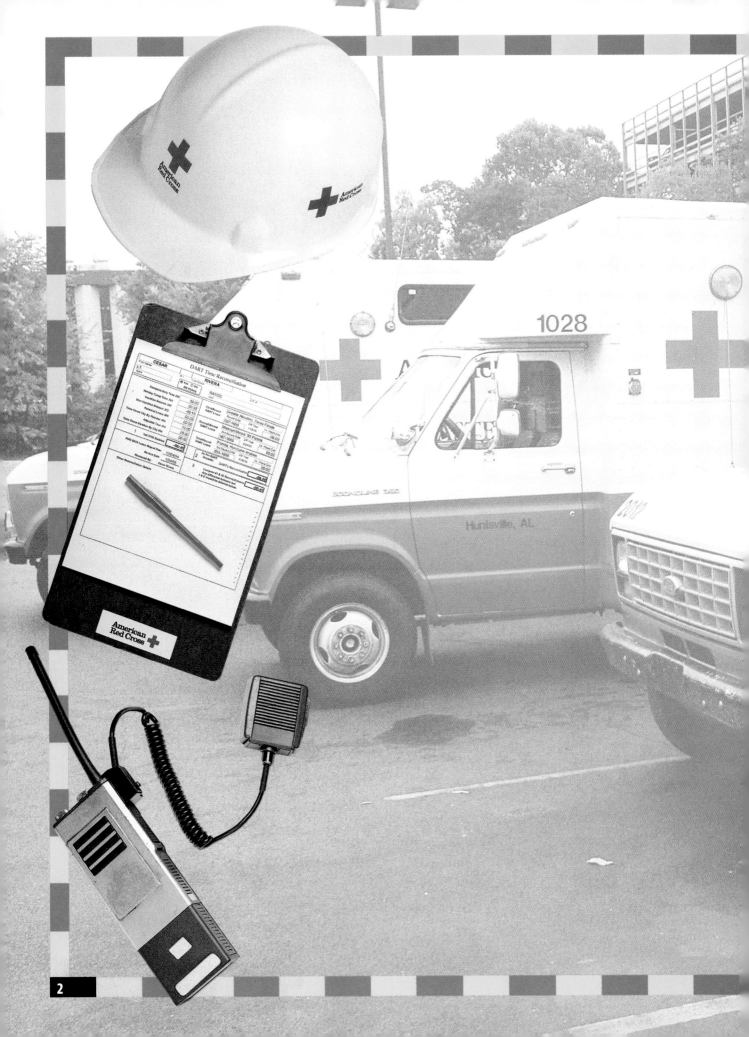

Observe

a Red Cross Station

Problem solving is a survival skill.

American Red Cross DISASTER SERVICES

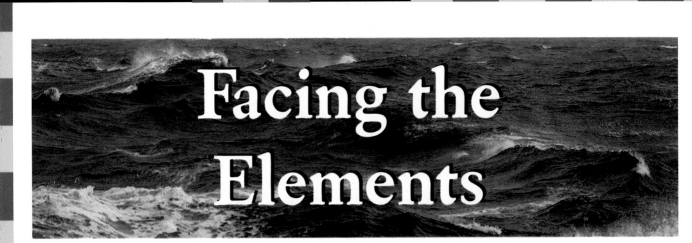

Facing the Elements

We learn to live in the natural world.

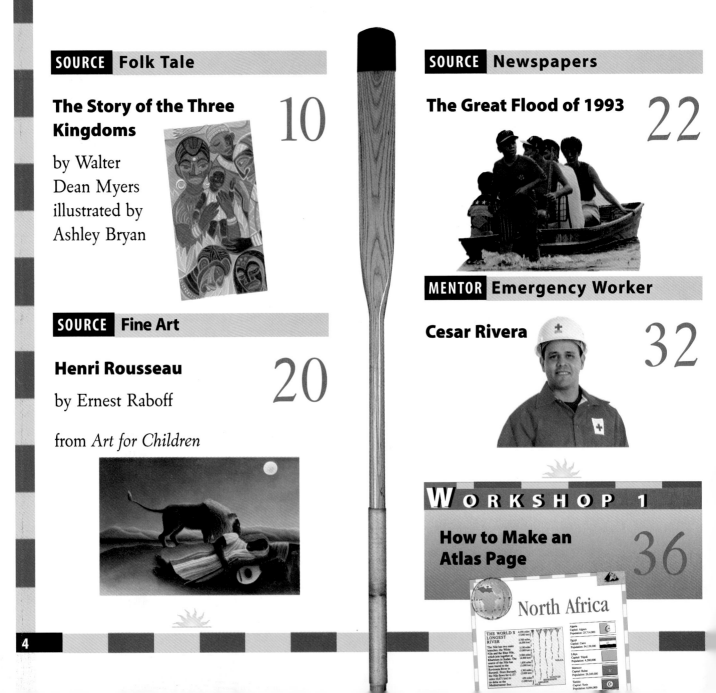

SOURCE Folk Tale

The Story of the Three Kingdoms   10

by Walter Dean Myers illustrated by Ashley Bryan

SOURCE Fine Art

Henri Rousseau   20

by Ernest Raboff

from *Art for Children*

SOURCE Newspapers

The Great Flood of 1993   22

MENTOR Emergency Worker

Cesar Rivera   32

WORKSHOP 1

How to Make an Atlas Page   36

North Africa

Accepting the Challenge

People solve problems as they confront the elements.

SOURCE Biography Collection

The Mountain That Refused to Be Climbed 42

by Doreen Rappaport

from *Living Dangerously*

SOURCE Atlas

from **Scholastic Atlas of Exploration** 60

by Dinah Starkey

SOURCE Novel

from **Black Star, Bright Dawn** 68

by Scott O'Dell
illustrated by Kong Lu

SOURCE Magazine

The Last Great Race 82

from *Scholastic Action*

W O R K S H O P 2

How to Compile an Equipment Checklist 86

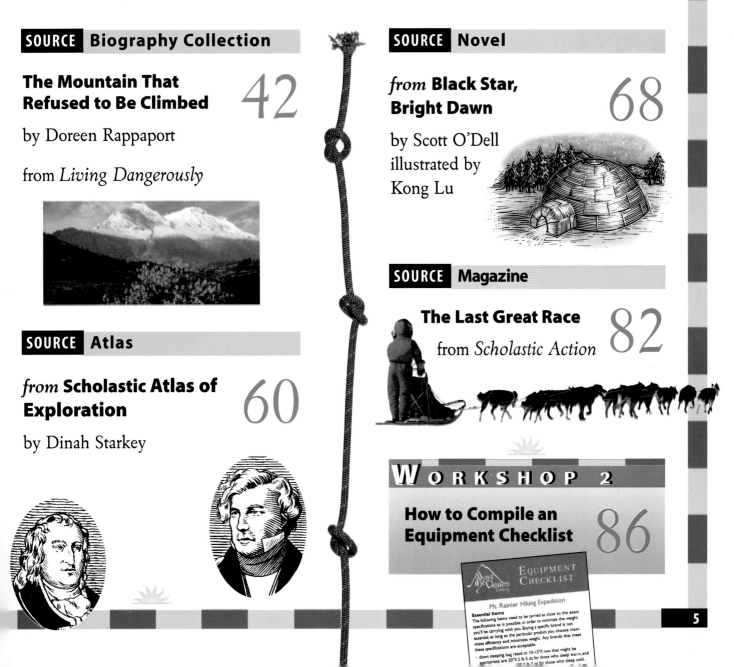

Tools of Survival

Knowledge and skills help people survive in new environments.

SOURCE Novel

from **Hatchet**
92
by Gary Paulsen
illustrated by Wayne McLoughlin

SOURCE Science Nonfiction

Wayfinding
108
by Vicki McVey
illustrated by Karen Minot

from *The Sierra Club Wayfinding Book*

SOURCE Poem

Staying Alive
126
by David Wagoner
illustrated by Danuta Jarecka

PROJECT

How to Write a Survival Guide
130

Glossary 136

Authors & Illustrators..........................140

Books & Media 142

Trade Books

The following books accompany this *Meet the Challenge* SourceBook.

Historical Fiction

The Big Wave

by Pearl S. Buck

Fiction

Island of the Blue Dolphins

by Scott O'Dell

Newbery Honor
Fiction

My Side of the Mountain

by Jean Craighead George

Fiction

The Ostrich Chase

by Moses L. Howard

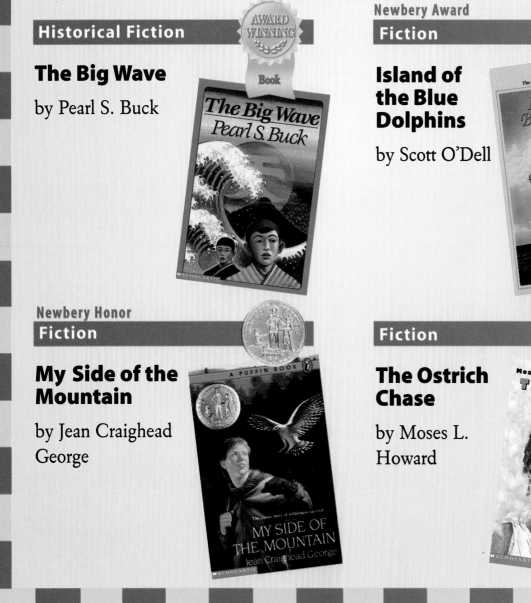

We learn to live
in the natural world.

Facing the Elements

Read a folk tale
about how
people and animals
learned to coexist
long ago. Then see
how this idea is
shown in art.

Find out how the
Midwest survived
the great flood
of 1993.

Meet Cesar Rivera,
who comes to the
rescue when natural
disasters strike.

WORKSHOP 1

Make an atlas
page describing
the challenges of
a particular
place.

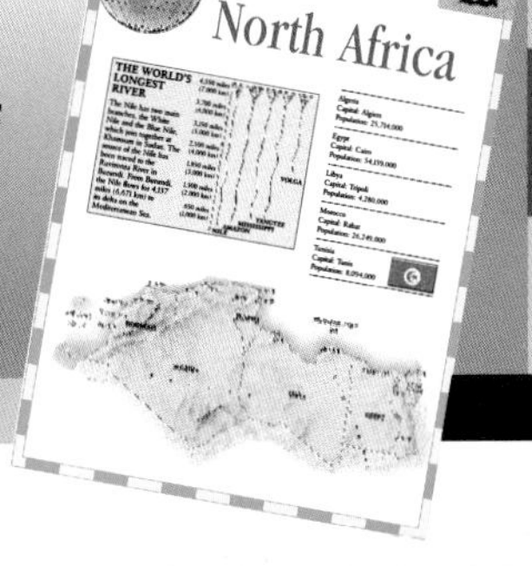

North Africa

9

THE STORY *of the* Three KINGDOMS

By Walter Dean Myers

Illustrated by Ashley Bryan

Long ago, when the earth had not settled in its turning and the stars had not found their places in the night sky, there were three kingdoms.

The first kingdom was that of the forest, and in the kingdom of the forest the giant Elephant ruled. When he spoke the trees trembled. When he walked the ground shook. No beast, great or small, dared to speak against him. No one would look into his great eye, for they were afraid to hurt his feelings.

"Mine is the greatest kingdom on earth," Elephant was fond of saying.

And as powerful as he was, many believed this to be true.

The second kingdom was that of the sea, and the ruler of the sea was Shark. Shark had many rows of sharp and shiny teeth that he bared in an angry glare. Fish both small and large would swim away when he came near. Lobsters would cover their mouths lest they speak a word that might be misunderstood.

"Mine is the greatest kingdom on earth," Shark would say from his home in the sea.

And since the sea covered most of the earth, many believed this to be true.

The third kingdom was that of the air, that wide place between heaven and earth, and it was Hawk who ruled the air. He soared through the skies each day with a great cry of "KAAAAAAA-AH! Kaaaaaa—AH!" Hawk had a great hooked beak and wickedly curved claws that he held ready as he soared swiftly on the wind.

When he flew, the thrush and the swallow would hide in the bushes.

"Mine is the greatest kingdom on earth," Hawk would call out from the skies. As much space as the sea held, the sky held more. Who was to deny that his kingdom was the greatest?

Elephant, Shark, and Hawk often argued among themselves.

"Come into my forest," said Elephant, "and let us test who is the strongest."

But Hawk and Shark would not go into the forest.

"Come into my sea," called Shark, "and I will teach you to obey me."

But neither Hawk nor Elephant would venture into the sea.

"Come into the air," Hawk cried, "and we will see who is master."

But neither Shark nor Elephant could lift themselves from the ground.

So it went, with each ruler thinking that his was the greatest kingdom and that he ruled the earth.

Then there came to earth some new creatures. They called themselves the People. They were not as strong as Elephant. They were not as fierce as Shark. Nor could they fly, like Hawk.

All of the other creatures in the forest, in the sea, and in the air laughed at the People.

"You are here to do our bidding," they all called out. And so it seemed. For many seasons the People walked with their chins upon their chests and their eyes cast down.

The People lived in the hills, not daring to go into the forest for fear that Elephant would crush them with his great strength.

Then it happened one day that Elephant fell into a great pit. Try as he might, he could not pull himself up. Nor was any other creature strong enough to pull him up. Many thought it was the end of Elephant.

But that night some of the People were sitting around a great fire. One spoke of something he had once seen. There had been a great stone in a place where the People wanted to build a village. The stone was too big for any one of the people to lift. But there were vines around the stone and some of the People pulled on them. With many of the People pulling on the vines the stone moved easily. Then the village was built.

This story was told and told again. The idea warmed in the minds of the People, and they knew it was good. The next day the People went to the pit. They tied many vines around Elephant and pulled him out. Elephant was grateful for their help.

"From this day on I will share the forest with you," said Elephant.

And so he did.

Another time it came to pass that Shark, with his terrible teeth, would not let the People bathe in the sea or take fish for their meals.

The People were sad as they sat around their fire. Then a woman told how her grandmother had woven a mat for her home. One day by chance she dropped it into a small brook. Lizard, swimming by, had caught himself in her weaving and could not escape. The People made the woman tell the story many times. They warmed the idea carefully in their minds, and knew it was good.

The next day the People wove the largest mat they could and threw it into the water. Into the net swam Shark, and he could not move.

"Let me loose!" Shark cried.

"Will you share the sea with us?" asked the People.

Shark turned and squirmed and gnashed his teeth, but he could not free himself from the net the People had woven.

"Let me loose," Shark cried, "and we will share the sea."

The People cut the mat and let Shark swim away. They never feared him again.

But Hawk, with his hooked beak and slashing claws, just laughed as he flew among the clouds.

"I am still ruler of the sky," he called. "And mine is the greatest kingdom!"

The People were afraid of Hawk, and they trembled when he flew above them.

But now the People knew what they could do. They gathered again around the fire and each told the stories they remembered. One told of watching a child trying to catch a butterfly. The child could not catch the butterfly as it flew, but caught it when it came to rest upon the ground.

This story, too, warmed in the minds of the People and they knew the idea was good. The next day the People went to the baobab tree where they knew Hawk came to rest. They waited, and when Hawk landed they threw a loop made from vines around him. Hawk screeched and flapped his wings, but he could not escape.

"Let me go," Hawk cried, "and I will share the air with you."

The People freed Hawk from the vines and no longer feared him.

"Now we are the masters of the earth," cried a young man. "We can rule the forest and make Elephant fear us! We can rule the sea and Shark will flee from us! We can rule the air and Hawk will tremble!"

But when the People gathered once again around the fire, telling the story of all that had happened, something new came to mind.

"We have overcome the strength of Elephant," they said, "and our fear of Shark and Hawk. We have done this by sitting by the fire and telling stories of what has happened to us, and learning from them. Only we, among all creatures, have the gift of story and the wisdom it brings. We do not need to be masters of the earth. We can share because it is wise to do so."

From that day on the People held their heads high, never forgetting to sit by the fire and tell their stories. Never forgetting that in the stories could be found wisdom and in wisdom, strength.

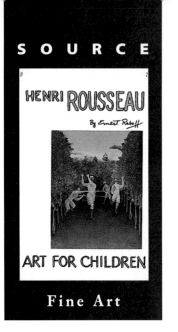
from
Art for Children by Ernest Raboff

HENRI ROUSSEAU

"THE SLEEPING GYPSY"

WAS DESCRIBED AS FOLLOWS BY
ROUSSEAU IN A LETTER:

"A WANDERING GYPSY WHO PLAYS THE MANDOLIN, WITH
HER JAR NEXT TO HER (A VASE CONTAINING DRINKING
WATER), IS DEEPLY ASLEEP, WORN OUT FROM FATIGUE.
A LION HAPPENS BY, SNIFFS AT HER, AND DOES NOT
DEVOUR HER. THERE IS AN EFFECT OF MOONLIGHT,
VERY POETIC. THE SCENE TAKES PLACE IN A
COMPLETELY ARID DESERT. . . ."

HENRI ROUSSEAU, LIKE HIS GYPSY, WAS A MUSICIAN
WHO WANDERED THE STREETS OF PARIS PLAYING HIS
VIOLIN.

HE WOULD PLAY HIS MUSIC AND PAINT HIS PICTURES
UNTIL HE WAS TOO TIRED TO CONTINUE. THEN HE
WOULD LIE DOWN AND SLEEP BELIEVING THAT HIS
LOVE FOR NATURE AND FOR LIFE WOULD ALWAYS
PROTECT HIM FROM ANY HARM.

20

THE SLEEPING GYPSY, 1897   MUSEUM OF MODERN ART, NEW YORK, GIFT OF MRS. SIMON GUGGENHEIM

From *The New York Times, The Kansas City Star,* and *The Des Moines Register*

The Great Flood of

1993

"A flood is an ugly thing to cover. You don't stand on the riverbank and get stories. You pull on waders, or climb in a boat, and live with and work with and sympathize with the people who are trying to survive."

—*Bill Wundram,* Quad-City Times, *Davenport, Iowa*

THE MISSISSIPPI river system is made up of the 2,340-mile-long Mississippi and its tributaries (the many rivers and streams that run into it). The waters drain most of the land between the Appalachian Mountains in the East and the Rocky Mountains in the West. If something goes wrong with so huge a system, its impact can be almost too great to calculate. In 1993, something went wrong.

_____

THE GREAT FLOOD of 1993 actually began in 1992. That spring, there had been a drought over most of the Midwest. By the Fourth of July weekend, the sky darkened; finally it rained. And rained. And rained. Freezing rain in the winter. And in the spring of '93, fierce thunderstorms.

_____

BY THE SUMMER of 1993, the mighty Mississippi had turned into a raging monster. Overflowing its banks for miles around, it carried away everything in its path. The people worked tirelessly to meet the challenge of the rising waters. Here are some of the news stories about the disaster that appeared at the time.

Along the Levee as People Fight a Tireless River

By SARA RIMER
Special to *The New York Times*

QUINCY, ILL. July 13—For 14 days now, through thunderstorms, sweltering heat, swarms of mosquitoes and never-ending mud, the people here have been working side by side around the clock in a war against the elements.

The troops are the National Guard, prison inmates, the county sheriff, local radio broad-casters, farmers, college students, construction workers, retirees, house-wives and even the Boy Scouts. Everyone but the National Guard is a volunteer in the battle against the Mississippi River.

Only lightning, which can strike the levee they are bolstering, stops them, but not for long. Those who aren't able to throw sandbags or drive bulldozers are cooking and delivering food for those who can.

Not Giving Up

The women of New Canton are washing the muddy clothes of the National Guardsmen. Everyone is worn out,

Volunteers checking the rising water at the levee in Fall Creek, Illinois.

but no one is giving up. Farmers here have already lost 41,000 acres of corn and soybeans, and tens of thousands more are at stake.

Susan Gooding has posted herself at the levee at Indian Grave. The man who farms the land just below it graduated from Quincy High School several years ahead of Ms. Gooding, who is 23. "Friday night, he was sitting down there on those sandbags," she said Monday night as she threw more sandbags against the levee. "He was so exhausted, he looked so defeated. He couldn't keep going. You just couldn't walk away and leave him."

To find the volunteers, one need only to follow the hand-printed cardboard signs posted along dirt roads in every town: "Levee Workers Needed. Sandbaggers. Help!" Or listen to the local radio station, WGEM, which is broadcasting a 24-hour flood watch.

People call in, pleading, "We need 200 sandbaggers at Snye's Landing." Or, "We need demolition trucks." Or boats. The radio announcers give directions on how to get there, and almost instantly, it seems, the 200 people, the trucks and the boats all appear.

At 9 A.M. today, 75 Illinois National Guardsmen were stretched out on their backs along one endangered levee north of Quincy. Their muddied boots were off, their life vests were beside them. At midnight, they had formed a human chain along the levee, throwing 30- and 40-pound sandbags, and they had gone until long past dawn.

An exhausted volunteer lay against a sandbag levee in West Des Moines, Iowa, as floodwaters rose.

What Is a Levee?

A levee is a wall that is built along the banks of a river to keep it from overflowing. The word levee comes from the French word lever, which means "to raise." In the United States, levees are made of sandbags and banked-up earth. The first levee built on the Mississippi River was constructed near the city of New Orleans in 1718. It was only three feet high. Today, levees measure anywhere from 15 to 30 feet high.

FROM

THE KANSAS CITY STAR

Tales of Valor, Fear and Kindness

July 10—For two hours, a tree in rural Douglas County became one of Cathy Johnson's dearest friends.

"It was about the only tree in the general area with branches low enough that we were able to climb up in it," Johnson said in a telephone interview.

Johnson, 44, and Candace Winter, 13, were inside a Pontiac Grand Prix about 5:10 A.M. when floodwaters swept the car off County Road 458 southeast of Lawrence. Somehow the tide spun the vehicle into the tree that saved them.

Johnson, who lives south of Kansas 10 between Lawrence and Eudora, had set out for Baldwin City with Candace, who was visiting from Minnesota. They were supposed to meet a woman in Baldwin City before continuing to Wichita to pick up Johnson's daughter from a cheerleading camp.

"I said to Candace, 'Help me watch for high water on the road.' It was raining so hard I couldn't see very far. We were going fairly slow, and neither one of us saw any water. Then, boom! We just hit and we started floating immediately," she said.

About 40 feet off the road, the Pontiac bumped against the tree and stopped.

Rainwater rushed in through the dashboard. Johnson felt her feet getting wet.

She and Candace scrambled for the back seat, but water kept coming in so loud that they could hear it. The electric car windows wouldn't budge. With a burst of adrenalin, they kicked open a back door.

Johnson grabbed a long, low-hanging branch and climbed onto the car trunk. She swung the branch back to Candace, who worked her way as high up in the tree as she could. They stood together in the chilly darkness and watched water slowly swamp the Pontiac.

They tried to remain calm.

"Believe it or not, we played the state capital game. We started with the A's and went all the way through the 50 states,"

DAYS OF RAIN From May 16 to July 15, rain was reported on 40 of 61 days.

MAY
16 17 18 19 20 21 22 23 24 25 26 27 28 29 30 31

JUNE
1 2 3 4 5 6 7 8 9 10 11 12 13 14 15

Source: Weatherdata, Inc.

The Flood's Legacy

	Deaths	Estimated property, crop damage	Number of evacuations	Number of homes damaged	Acreage flooded	Counties declared federal disaster areas
Illinois	1	More than $1 billion	15,000 people	7,200	875,000	35
Iowa	7	$3.5 billion	12,610 families	13,335	2.2 million	99
Minnesota	4	$1 billion	1,100 families	10,000	5 million	48
Missouri	25	More than $3 billion	19,000 people	12,000	more than 3 million	79
Nebraska	1	$377 million	247 people	2,000	5.8 million	90
South Dakota	4	$738 million	2,000 people	745	3.6 million	37
Wisconsin	2	$800 million to $1 billion	2,500 people	4,700	Not available	46
Kansas	1	More than $475 million	13,000 people	3,414	4.6 million	46
North Dakota	2	$520 million	100 people	4,500	9.4 million	37

The Star

Source: State governors' offices and the Federal Emergency Management Agency

Johnson said. "Then I sang her a couple of stupid songs. One of them was, 'It Ain't Going to Rain No More, No More.' She didn't cry. She didn't panic."

About an hour later, Johnson saw headlights down the road. They belonged to the car of a Douglas County sheriff's deputy. The deputy hit the wall of water and backed up. Johnson and Candace started hollering for help.

At 7:15 a.m. the tree sitters finally were out.

"There was a moment in the car when I didn't think we were going to get out," Johnson said. "And I can't swim, to top it all off…It was a good thing we had each other."

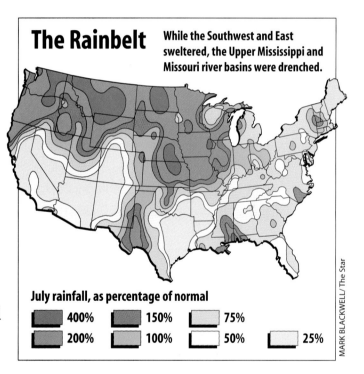

The Rainbelt

While the Southwest and East sweltered, the Upper Mississippi and Missouri river basins were drenched.

July rainfall, as percentage of normal

- 400%
- 200%
- 150%
- 100%
- 75%
- 50%
- 25%

MARK BLACKWELL / The Star

| 16 | 17 | 18 | 19 | 20 | 21 | 22 | 23 | 24 | 25 | 26 | 27 | 28 | 29 | 30 | **JULY** 1 | 2 | 3 | 4 | 5 | 6 | 7 | 8 | 9 | 10 | 11 | 12 | 13 | 14 | 15 |

DAVE EAMES / The Star

From

The Des Moines Register

Teens Find It's Fun to Make a Difference

Jim Beach, 19, figured he ripped open about 1 million boxes at the Salvation Army's Flood Disaster Distribution Center Saturday.

That might be a slight exaggeration, he admitted. But he added, "I know we did thousands."

Five hours of hauling and tearing open boxes left him bruised and smudged with dirt, but also profoundly moved at the generosity of people in faraway places such as New York, Oklahoma and Florida, who took time to send supplies to Iowans they've never met.

Beach and about 30 other teenagers from Greene left their small town in north-central Iowa about dawn Saturday morning. They are members of the Greene Teen Betterment Council, a group that works to improve their town. Saturday they came to help Des Moines.

"Everyone is the same, basically," said Beach, a 1993 graduate. "They feel good helping other people."

The Greene teens spent more than 10 hours helping at the center, scheduled to open today at the former Target store on Fleur Drive.

It doesn't matter that they'll never meet the

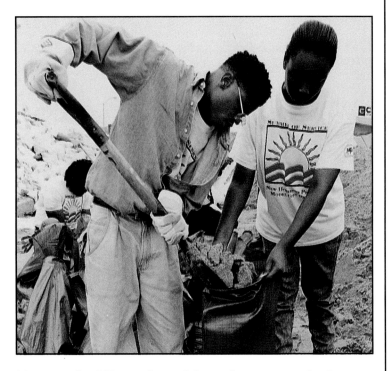

Two youths filling a bag with sand to use on the levee.

people they came to help, Beach said.

"What if we hadn't been here today? All this stuff would still be here, but now it's done," he said. "We know personally what we've done."

Watching the activity, Beach said he realized the country is not as bad off as some say.

"I'm just amazed that people can pull together like this," he said.

Young workers packed the distribution center, helping unload and sort all kinds of items—from baby formula to dog food, from sponges to furniture—that will be given free to flood victims.

"Let me tell you, it's exciting," Salvation Army Maj. Irene Rubin said. "Kids have a lot of energy," she said. "They're going to spend it somewhere."

Young workers filled hundreds of plastic bags with necessities, such as toilet paper, paper plates and cups. In the afternoon, they tossed bag after bag near the center of the room.

The scene was familiar. A pile quickly grew far above the youths' heads. It looked like a big pink-and-white plastic levee.

With a rope around his waist and attached to the boat, Brad Christiansen, 10, ferries residents down their flooded street.

Coping With Disaster

The Great Flood of '93 as seen through the lens of a camera, a child's drawing, and the work of a cartoonist.

A man braves the rising flood waters to rescue his cat.

The Flood of '93 came as fast and high as a giant tidal wave leaving behind no safe water to drink for over a month and it left many memories.

— Kirk Piltingsrud,
Weeks Middle School

The Flood of '93

In many areas of the Midwest, the U.S. Coast Guard was called in to help locate and rescue stranded flood victims.

In Missouri, two young volunteers help build a sandbag levee.

How do people best deal with disaster? With hard work, patience, courage, and—as the cartoon above shows—a sense of humor.

Cesar Rivera

Emergency Worker

He's always *ready* to lend *a* helping hand.

In 1989, Hurricane Hugo slammed into Puerto Rico and the east coast of the U.S. When the devastating winds let up, the American Red Cross called for help. Cesar Rivera and 16 other members of the New York City Fire Department promptly gave up their vacation time to help out. That experience led Rivera to form a Disaster Assistance Response Team—DART. Today, when disaster strikes, Rivera and his DART volunteers are on the job.

PROFILE

Name: Cesar Rivera

Occupation: full-time firefighter; part-time emergency volunteer for the Red Cross

Education: DeWitt Clinton High School, New York City

Hobby: running to relieve tension

Most important part of his job: providing compassion and support for disaster victims

Fire Department   City of New York

CERTIFICATE OF APPRECIATION

PRESENTED TO

Lt. Cesar Rivera

for your dedication above and beyond the call of duty through the Disaster Assistance Response Team. You have extended the New York City Fire Department's proud tradition of service to victims of disasters here and across the United States.

October 28, 1994

N.Y.C. World Trade Center Fire, 1993
N.Y.C. Blizzard, 1993
Midwest Floods, 1993

Howard Safir
Fire Commissioner

QUESTIONS
for Cesar Rivera

Here's how **a volunteer** worker **tackles** an emergency.

 What do you and your DART volunteers do when you're called into a disaster situation?

A By the time we arrive on the scene, nature has done its worst, and the immediate danger has passed. We help get food and shelter for people who need them, and sometimes we help rebuild homes that are damaged.

Q **What kinds of disaster situations have you been called to?**

A Since Hurricane Hugo, we've been called out over 100 times. We spent three weeks in Florida after Hurricane Andrew hit. We went to Missouri after the flooding there. Some of us went out to Los Angeles after the earthquake.

 What's the biggest challenge you face when you enter situations like those?

 I think it's the challenge of solving unexpected problems. And during a disaster operation, something unexpected always happens.

 Can you give an example?

 When we were in St. Louis, Missouri, after the floods, the stock of food supplies was kept outside because there was nowhere else to store it. Some supplies were ruined when it rained, and cans of food were exploding because it was too hot. Morale was low because it seemed like there was no solution to the problem. It's terrible when people lose hope in a disaster situation.

American Red Cross DISASTER SERVICES

Q **What did you do?**

A We had to come up with a new way to protect the supplies from the sun and the rain. We went to a construction supply company nearby, got some materials, and rigged up a tent. It worked! We took care of a problem that had been haunting us for a few weeks. We solved two problems at once: the practical problem of protecting the supplies, and the morale problem. Everyone was so proud of that tent.

Q **Is communication important in a disaster situation?**

A It's very important. If communication systems break down, you won't get the support you need to handle the situation. When we first approach a disaster scene, we determine how many people or homes are affected so we know how much help to bring in.

Q **What happens when communication is impossible?**

A In Florida after Hurricane Andrew, the phone system broke down. That's when improvisation came into play. We used ham radios and other alternative forms of communication to exchange information.

Cesar Rivera's
Tips for an Emergency Situation

1 Remain calm.

2 Stay focused on the problem at hand—don't let your mind wander.

3 Find an adult to help you, and/or call an emergency number, such as 911. Tell the person your location, and what the problem is.

How to
Make an Atlas Page

What makes one landscape different from another? One place may have jagged, icy mountain peaks while another may have acres of dense, mysterious rain forest. How do travelers discover the geographical features of a place they want to visit? They often turn to a page in an atlas that will tell them about the place.

What is an atlas page? An atlas page consists of information about a geographical location. It includes a map and facts about the area, such as the length of a river, the height of a mountain peak, or the population. Because an atlas page provides such important information about the geographical features of an area, it can help travelers anticipate problems and prepare for them.

The title of the page tells the name of the place. ●•••••

An important feature may be highlighted. ●•

Cities and towns are represented by a symbol.●••

Natural ● features are shown.

North Africa

THE WORLD'S LONGEST RIVER

The Nile has two main branches, the White Nile and the Blue Nile, which join together at Khartoum in Sudan. The source of the Nile has been traced to the Ruvironza River in Burundi. From Burundi, the Nile flows for 4,137 miles (6,671 km) to its delta on the Mediterranean Sea.

4,350 miles (7,000 km)

3,700 miles (6,000 km)

3,150 miles (5,000 km)

2,500 miles (4,000 km)

1,850 miles (3,000 km)

1,300 miles (2,000 km)

650 miles (1,000 km)

VOLGA

YANGTZE
MISSISSIPPI
AMAZON
NILE

Algeria
Capital: Algiers
Population: 25,714,000

Egypt
Capital: Cairo
Population: 54,139,000

Libya
Capital: Tripoli
Population: 4,280,000

Morocco
Capital: Rabat
Population: 26,249,000

Tunisia
Capital: Tunis
Population: 8,094,000

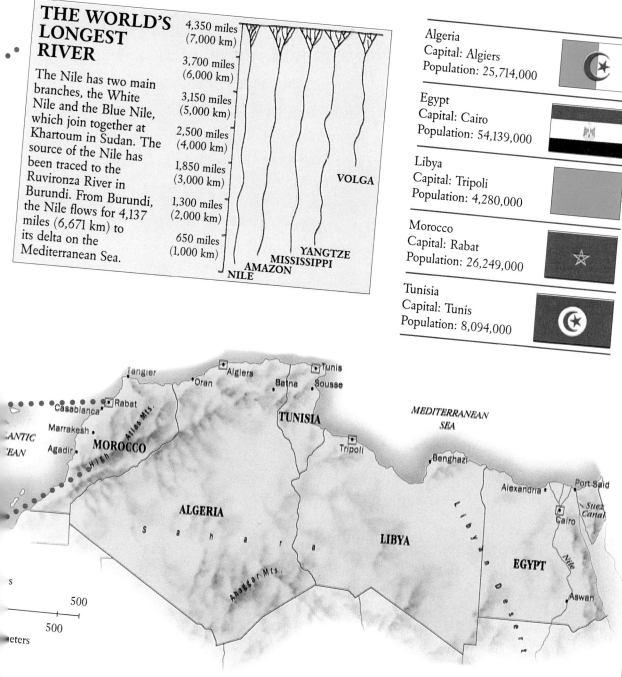

1 Choose a Place

What places capture your imagination? Make a list of at least five places you'd like to explore. You might use a globe or an atlas to help you with your list. Your choice could be a large area, such as Antarctica, or a smaller one, such as Yellowstone National Park. It could be a country, such as Indonesia, or a specific natural region—the Andes Mountains, for example. From your list of possibilities, choose one place you'd like to learn more about.

TOOLS

- reference books
- magazines
- pencil and paper
- ruler
- markers

2 Do Research

Use books and magazines to find out as much as you can about the place you've chosen. Gather information about the climate, wildlife, and population. Think about the kinds of challenges or problems a traveler might face. If your location is a mountain range, should travelers be on the lookout for avalanches? If it is in a tropical region, do hurricanes happen during certain seasons of the year? Is there a particular species of poisonous snake or insect that lives there? What kinds of information would help a traveler to explore the region?

3 Review Information

Gather your notes and pictures together and decide which information you want to include on your atlas page. What are the most important facts? What information would be most helpful to someone unfamiliar with the area? Decide what features should be pictured on your map. Choose the areas on your map that you want to highlight, such as a volcano or a piranha-infested river. You might want to create a table that shows the average rainfall and temperature of your area.

Tip See if you can get some photographs of your place to add to your atlas page. Travel brochures and magazines are good sources.

4 Organize and Present

After you have collected all your material, decide how to organize your information on an atlas page. You'll want to have a good balance of words and pictures. Draw your map in pencil before coloring it in. Label important places and include the information you decided would be helpful to others. Remember to use the name of your place as the title of your atlas page. Then share your atlas page with the rest of your class.

If You Are Using a Computer...

Use the Newsletter format to create your atlas page. Remember to leave room for photographs, which you can paste on your atlas page after it's printed out. Browse through the clip art library for maps and illustrations.

THINK

Where else might a traveler find information that will help anticipate and prevent problems?

Cesar Rivera
Emergency Worker ▶

People solve problems as they confront the elements.

Accepting the Challenge

Find out how mountain climber Annie Smith Peck battled the forces of nature. Learn more about others who challenged nature.

Experience the thrill of the Alaskan Iditarod in a story about a young girl and her sled dogs. Discover the real-life story of a dogsled-racing champion.

WORKSHOP 2

Compile a list of equipment you would need on a trip to a new place.

EQUIPMENT CHECKLIST

Mt. Rainier Hiking Expedition

Essential Items
The following items need to be carried as close to the exact specifications as is possible, in order to minimize the weight you'll be carrying with you. Buying a specific brand is not essential, as long as the particular product you choose meets sizes efficiency and minimum weight. Any brands that meet these specifications are acceptable.

- down sleeping bag rated to 10–15°F, ones that might be appropriate are 20°F, 2 lb. 1 oz for those who sleep warm, and a heavier version at 5°F, 3 lb 3 oz for those who sleep cold. We strongly recommend getting a compression stuff sack to save room.
- small flashlight or head lamp (5 oz with 2 AA batteries)
- warm, water-resistant thermal ski jacket weighing 1 lb 6 oz
- warm, water-resistant thermal ski pants weighing 1 lb 2 oz
- waterproof rain slicker
- one cotton t-shirt
- one wool or flannel long sleeve shirt
- one pair of lightweight outdoor trousers
- two pairs thin liner socks made of polypropylene or silk
- one pair heavy Norwegian rag-wool outer socks
- lightweight hiking boots or well-broken-in leather hiking boots
- warm gloves
- duckbill baseball cap or Alpine hat
- one-liter water bottle
- personal medications, including prescription drugs, lip balm, lotion
- toiletries, all in compact, lightweight varieties (brush, tooth paste, soap)
- medium-sized pack with rain cover to contain all of the above

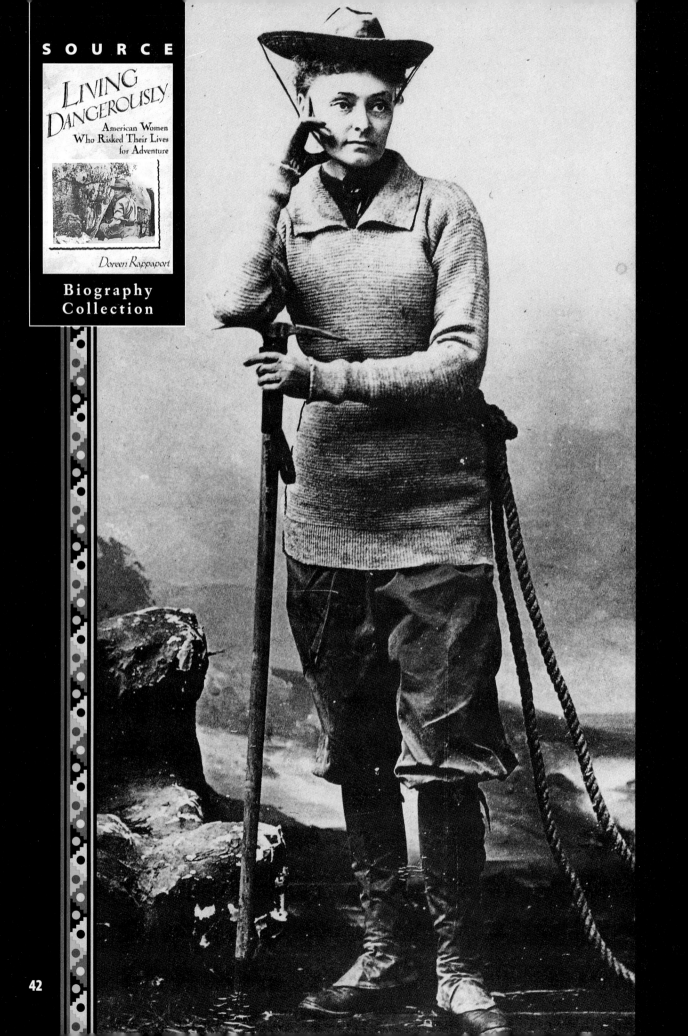

LIVING
DANGEROUSLY

American Women
Who Risked Their Lives
for Adventure

Doreen Rappaport

Biography
Collection

From
LIVING DANGEROUSLY
American Women Who Risked Their Lives for Adventure

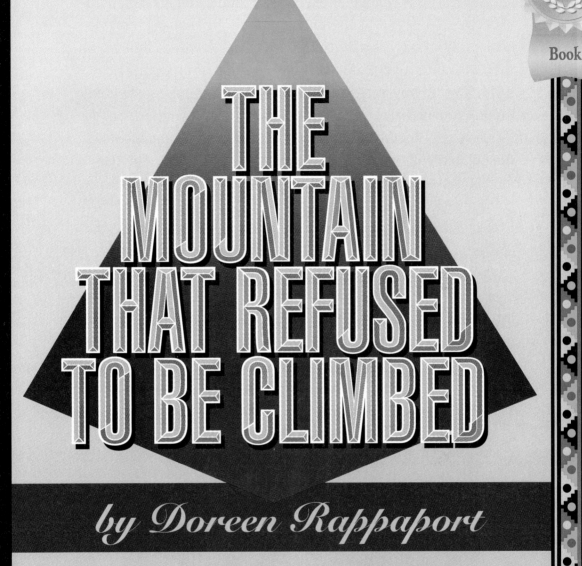

THE MOUNTAIN THAT REFUSED TO BE CLIMBED

by Doreen Rappaport

AWARD WINNING

Book

Friday, August 28 – Saturday, September 5, 1908
Yungay, Peru

ANNIE SMITH PECK pushed open the shutters and leaned out the window. She looked past the square in Yungay's center, down a narrow dirt road lined by red-roofed houses, past the fields of wheat and corn, up to the snowcapped twin peaks of Huascarán, the highest mountain in Peru. It was a maze of snow and ice at over 22,000 feet (6,700 meters) above sea level. No one had ever climbed it to the top.

Huascarán is shaped like a horse's saddle. Thousands of feet of rocky slopes lead to an immense glacier that spans the twin peaks. The glacier is a moving mass of ice. Anyone climbing it may encounter dangerous crevasses—deep fissures that drop suddenly into abysses—and snow avalanches that unexpectedly thunder down.

Climate is another danger. Ice-cold winds batter the mountain. At such high altitudes there is less oxygen to breathe. The body's metabolism slows down. Every step tests a person's physical endurance to its limits. No wonder no one had ever reached the top.

In the last four years Annie had tried five times to scale these snowy peaks and icy crags, and five times she had failed. Her last attempt had been only ten days ago.

People constantly asked her why she pursued this dangerous, impossible dream. Annie didn't try to make them understand. She didn't think that people who viewed mountains from valleys or from railroad trains could ever understand the beauty and power of those white-domed peaks floating toward the deep blue of the sky, belonging more to heaven than to earth.

Mount Huascarán, the highest mountain in Peru.

But it wasn't only the beauty of mountains that attracted Annie. Ever since childhood Annie had taken on challenges. As the youngest child and only girl among three brothers, she had learned not to be intimidated by men's supposedly superior physical strength and endurance. When her brothers refused to let her join them in their games, she practiced until she was as good as they were, if not better. When her brothers went off to college, Annie vowed she would go too, even though there were only a few women's colleges and fewer coed colleges at that time. In 1874 she gained admission to the University of Michigan. She majored in Greek and excelled in every subject she studied. But earning a college degree wasn't enough for Annie. She went on to get a master's in Greek and became one of the first women college professors in the United States.

Annie and her oldest brother scaled California's Mount Shasta in 1888.

In 1885, on a trip through Switzerland, Annie saw the 14,690 foot (4,478 meter) Matterhorn, and her passion for the classics started to give way to a passion for mountain climbing. She became determined to scale its "frowning walls." She prepared by climbing smaller mountains in Greece and Switzerland. In 1888 she and her oldest brother scaled California's 14,162 foot (4,316 meter) Mount Shasta. In 1895 she became the third woman to conquer the Matterhorn.

Annie was the third woman in the world to climb the Matterhorn in Switzerland.

Annie Smith Peck dressed like a lady, but she refused to wear a long skirt when mountain climbing. Instead, she wore the clothes pictured below.

She became instantaneously famous. People marveled at the endurance and courage of this woman, forty-five years old and barely five feet tall. Her climbing outfit—a hip-length tunic, short pants, high boots and a canvas hat tied with a veil under her chin—created as much of a sensation as her daring achievement. How unladylike, men said, and many women agreed. But Annie refused to wear floor-length skirts like other women climbers. It was ridiculous and dangerous to dress "like a lady."

Annie's triumph over the Matterhorn propelled her on. She gave up teaching and became a full-time climber, supporting herself by lecturing about her adventures. By 1900, having achieved over twenty successful climbs, she was recognized as one of the world's foremost climbers in a field still considered a man's sport.

But that wasn't enough for Annie either. She became determined to conquer a mountain no man had ever conquered. That mountain was Huascarán.

ANNIE closed the shutters, picked up her clothing sack and a heavy wool poncho and went downstairs. The four porters were carrying the expedition equipment outside. One sack held the ice axes, climbing irons, poles and ropes. Annie's lightweight silk tent and the sleeping bags were rolled up in the corner. The kerosene stove and kettles filled a third sack. Food was in a fourth bag. In a fifth bag were Annie's camera and a hypsometer, which she would use to measure the altitude at the top of Huascarán to establish its exact height.

Peruvian porters like this one accompanied Annie on her expeditions.

Annie gave her clothing and poncho to one of the men. As temperatures dropped on the climb, she would eventually wear everything in the sack: two woolen face masks, fur mittens, black woolen sleeves, three suits of lightweight wool underwear, two pairs of tights, two pairs of woolen stockings, knickers, two flannel shirts, a jacket and two sweaters. Her hiking boots were big and clumsy. They had to be four sizes larger than her regular shoes to accommodate the heavy stockings.

Unfortunately none of her clothing was water- or windproof. Admiral Peary, the famous Arctic explorer, had lent her a waterproof Eskimo suit, but on her last climb it had fallen irretrievably out of a porter's hands into a crevasse.

She went outside. Her guides, Gabriel Zumtaugwald and Rudolf Taugwalder, were supervising the packing of supplies on the horses. Like other expert climbers, Annie favored Swiss guides. They knew so much about snow and rock that they always chose the most practical and safe paths even when in unfamiliar territory.

Gabriel and Rudolf were skilled but stubborn, and impatient whenever Annie made suggestions—even though she was their employer and knew the mountain better than they did. They wouldn't listen when she suggested they wear at least two pairs of wool stockings. Her guides of two years ago, wearing two pairs

of stockings, had barely escaped losing their toes to frostbite. They didn't like taking advice from a woman.

The party set off on horseback for the three-hour ride to the copper mines, where they would rest overnight before hiking to the snow line. The horses trotted down the narrow walled road out of the village and soon ascended to where the houses became more scattered. The air was fragrant with blossoms of yellow broom and blue larkspur. Fields of wheat and corn blanketed the landscape with deep yellows. On the mountain snow was falling. An occasional villager, bent from years of working in the fields, passed them on the road.

When they arrived at the mines, Annie felt faint and a bit sick. She didn't know why. The ride had been easy enough. She ate a small bowl of soup and two boiled eggs and lay down to take a nap. But sleep did not come easily.

This typical Peruvian mountain village is similar to those Annie and her party passed through on their way to Mt. Huascarán.

When Annie saw clouds over the mountain the next morning, she postponed the ascent. The fresh snow needed at least another day of melting by the sun and freezing at night to make the mountain suitable for climbing.

At eight A.M. the next day they set out for the snow line. The walking was easy. Within six hours, they reached the first campsite, set up their tents, had soup and tea, and went to bed at sunset.

Admiral Peary, the famous Arctic explorer

49

For steep and difficult ice climbing, crampons (a pronged, skate-like device) are strapped onto boots.

By seven the following morning they were at the glacier. The porters put climbing irons over their shoes to bite into the surface of snow and ice. Annie and the guides wore boots studded with nails. Annie's studs weren't as pointed as her guides', but she didn't want to wear climbing irons. On the last ascent the strap on one of Annie's irons had been too tight. It had hindered her circulation. Two of her toes and the top of her right foot had gotten slightly frostbitten.

The climbing continued to be easy. Annie's instinct to wait the extra day had been right. The snow was easy to walk on. In seven hours they were well up in the saddle of the mountain. They pitched their tent under a snow wall. But despite the wall's shelter, a chilling wind swept through the tent all night.

There was no wind the next morning, but the air was thin and bitter cold. Annie thought it was the coldest day she had ever experienced on the mountain in all her climbs.

The ascent became radically steeper. Gabriel went first, probing for crevasses with his pickaxe and cutting small zigzag steps up the almost perpendicular wall. Annie, tied to a rope with Rudolf and a porter named Lucas, followed, pushing her pole into the glassy surface. The pole's pointed iron provided leverage, but the climbing was difficult and exhausting.

An hour later they reached a bridge of ice over a crevasse. Annie hesitated to cross it because there was no way to tell how strong it was. Rudolf crawled quickly over it on his hands and knees, then sat on the other side and wound the rope, still tied to Annie and the porter, around his ice axe to anchor it. Annie

hurried across next, then knotted her length of rope around her ice axe. Lucas was carrying too much on his back to hurry across. He stepped cautiously onto the ice bridge and suddenly slipped off the bridge and disappeared into the crevasse. Annie heard his cry as she gripped the rope more firmly to keep from being pulled over with him.

"Quick, quick." Gabriel, tied to the other three porters on a second rope, motioned for the porters to untie themselves. He threw their rope down to Lucas, who—though hanging head down—managed to tie it to his own rope and miraculously turn himself upright. He tugged on the rope. Annie and the men pulled him up. Annie was relieved to see him, but was dismayed to see that his pack, with the new stove in it, was not with him. They

couldn't go on without the stove.

"I'll go down for it," Gabriel said, and within seconds he was lowered down on a rope. Annie was worried. They were at least 19,000 feet above sea level. Exerting oneself at this height was dangerous. And maybe it was a fool's errand. There was no telling how deep the crevasse was or if Gabriel could even find the pack.

Annie and her party used an ice bridge to help them cross a crevasse, but sometimes climbers have to rely on only their ropes.

She waited impatiently. Ten minutes later Gabriel pulled on the rope. They hauled him up. The pack, with the stove in it, was in his hands.

They moved on. By dark they were at the top of the saddle. Tomorrow, with any luck, she would reach the top. *Finally, after all these years.*

Winds battered the tent all night and were so fierce the next morning that Annie suggested postponing the final climb until the wind died down.

"It's too dangerous," she said, "and we need rest." She was exhausted from the last two days and knew that the men had to be too, even though they wouldn't admit it.

"It'll be less windy higher up," countered Rudolf.

"I know this mountain," Annie argued. "Unless the wind dies down altogether, it'll be worse higher up."

"I think Rudolf's right," said Gabriel. "We should go on."

Annie yielded reluctantly. They agreed to leave the porters behind.

She was wearing every stitch of clothing she had packed but the poncho. She didn't want to put it on yet. It was too clumsy. She slipped a mask over her face and neck and put on her fur mittens. Rudolf put on his face mask. Gabriel didn't have a

Annie wore a mask over her face and neck in extremely cold conditions.

Mountain climbers nearing the summit of Mt. Huascarán

mask. Annie offered him her extra one and was surprised when he graciously accepted it.

"Could one of you carry my poncho?" This was asking a big favor, for at this altitude every extra bit of weight was a strain.

Rudolf acted as if he didn't hear her. "I'll do it," said Gabriel, even though he was already burdened with the food sack and the bag with hypsometer and camera.

Within an hour of climbing the sun was higher in the sky and Annie's hands were sweating inside the fur mittens. She took off her fur mittens and exchanged them for two pairs of woolen mittens in Rudolf's sack. One pair did not cover the fingers.

Up, up, the climbing was slow and strenuous. The cold winds had blown away the lighter snow on the surface, and the glacier was like glass.

"I've never seen such large patches of ice on any mountain in Switzerland," Rudolf said.

"I told you Huascarán is the fiercest mountain in the world," Annie said proudly.

They turned a ridge, and the wind knifed through Annie. She took her poncho from Gabriel. She needed her fur mittens. They stopped, and Rudolf opened his sack.

"Which ones first?" he asked, tucking Annie's wool sleeves and fur mittens under his right arm.

Hold on to them tight, Annie thought, but she didn't say it. "The sleeves."

Rudolf reached under his arm, but the wind got there first. Annie watched a fur mitten blow over the precipice. She was furious. There was no way to retrieve it. The woolen gloves would never be warm enough, and now her hands would probably get frostbitten.

Rudolf apologized. Annie ignored the apology. She hastily put the one fur mitten on over the other gloves on her right hand, which carried her pickaxe. It was more exposed to the cold than the left hand.

Up, up. The air was so thin, Annie had trouble breathing. It became harder and harder to move her legs. It was even hard pushing the pickaxe into the icy surface.

They stopped to eat. The meat and bread had frozen in the sack, but it didn't matter. They were too tired to eat much anyway. They nibbled on chocolate and raisins and drank the partially frozen tea in Rudolf's canteen.

"I'm too tired to go any farther," Rudolf announced.

Annie didn't want to stop. They were probably only an hour away from the top. *So close now!* "You can rest and we'll go ahead," she said to Rudolf.

"No let's all rest for an hour and then go on," said Gabriel. Annie agreed reluctantly.

The hour's rest did little to revive them. When they started climbing again, the cold, thin air was so debilitating that they had to stop frequently.

At three P.M. they rounded the final rise leading to the top of the mountain. The wind was stronger than ever. Annie's left hand felt numb. She pulled off her mitten and saw that the hand was nearly black. She rubbed her fingers vigorously with snow to revive the circulation. The rubbing made her fingers ache, a good sign that they weren't frostbitten. She tucked her hands inside the poncho, grateful for its length.

"We'd better measure the altitude now," said Gabriel. "It may be too windy at the top."

They untied themselves from each other. Rudolf wandered off, but Annie paid no attention. She was too busy shielding the hypsometer from the wind as Gabriel struck one match after another, hoping to light the candles so they could boil the water. A hypsometer is an instrument that is able to determine altitude in relation to the boiling point of water, which decreases as altitude increases. Annie wanted to know exactly how high she was and whether she had set a world's record.

She looked around for Rudolf. *Where is he? Maybe if he helped, we could get the candles lit.* After twenty tries, they gave up. Annie was disappointed. Now she could only estimate how high the mountain really was.

"We'd better move on to the top. It's half past three," said Gabriel.

Annie looked around for Rudolf again.

Suddenly he appeared. "I've been to the top," he said.

How dare he steal the honor? He wouldn't have dared do this if I were a man. Just an hour ago he wanted to quit. And he hasn't done half as much work as Gabriel. The guides knew she expected, as was the tradition, that as organizer of the expedition she would be the first to place her foot on the top of the mountain.

I won't tell him now how mad I am, but if we get down alive, I'll tell him. If we get down alive... The thought frightened her.

She set out for the top without a word. The winds battered her, and several times she had to stop and lean on her pickaxe to catch her breath.

"Don't go too near the edge," warned Gabriel, stepping aside to let her arrive first on the top of the mountain.

I'm here after all these years. She wanted to shout for joy, but there was no time to waste. Soon it would be dark. It had taken seven hours to climb to the top. How long would it take to go down? Steep rocks and icy slopes were far more dangerous to descend than to climb. She hurriedly photographed the views on all sides.

They tied themselves together again. Rudolf led, cutting the steps. Annie was in the middle, Gabriel at the rear. Their lives depended on Gabriel. If they slipped and he couldn't hold the rope to stop their fall, all three could plunge to death.

They turned a ridge and confronted a sixty-degree slope. "Be careful," said Gabriel.

Something black flew by.

"What is it?" Annie cried.

"One of my mittens," said Rudolf. "I took it off to fasten my shoe."

Rudolf worked fast, cutting the steps the size of toeholds. Small steps were fine going up, but dangerous going down. Annie zigzagged her way down the steep slope. There was nothing to hold on to. She wished she had her climbing irons now. She needed that kind of grip on this glassy surface.

She missed a step and slid three feet. Gabriel's strong hands held the rope tightly, and she regained her footing. A few seconds later she missed another step and slipped again. She was about to yell, "It's not serious," when she slid again. Five, ten, fifteen feet down the incline. Again Gabriel's strong hands checked her fall.

"Get up," he yelled, but the rope was twisted so tightly around her waist that she couldn't move. The men came to her and hauled her up.

The summit of Mt. Huascarán

They moved on. Her poncho, swaying wide in the wind, constantly hid her view of her next step. Down, down she stepped. Again she slipped. Her fall pulled Rudolf down, too. Gabriel's strong hands checked both their falls.

I don't think we'll make it down alive. It's too dark and too slippery. And I'm so tired.

She slid again and again. She tried to convince herself that they would make it down alive.

She lost track of how much time was passing as she concentrated on each step. She wasn't even aware, three hours later, that they were on the gentler slope just over the campsite until Gabriel shouted, "We're safe. Now you can slide if you like."

Annie laughed. They untied themselves from each other and dragged their tired bodies toward the tent. It was half past ten. They were too tired to eat and almost too tired to lie down. But safety felt good.

In the tent Annie noticed both of Rudolf's hands were black. "Rub them hard," she said. But Rudolf was so weak, he couldn't do it. *I'll do it,* thought Annie, but she was too tired to do it. *I'll get a porter to do it.* But in her tiredness, she forgot.

Peruvian porters, like the ones pictured here, helped Annie and her party down the mountain.

The three climbers huddled together on one side of the tent across from the porters. Annie wrapped the blankets around herself and the two men. When she realized the middle was the warmest spot, she moved to the outside and let Rudolf be in the center.

When they awakened the next morning, the wind was fierce. They were too exhausted to complete the rest of the trip down the mountain. By Thursday the wind had abated, and feeling more rested, they started down the mountain. They arrived at the mine two days later, on Saturday morning, September 5, about 10 A.M. After breakfast, they returned to Yungay.

—————————

Becoming the first person to climb to the top of Huascarán brought Annie world fame. The Peruvian government gave her a gold medal. In 1928 the Lima Geographical Society named the north peak of Huascarán Ana Peck. But Annie's triumph over Huascarán was marred for her by the subsequent amputation of Rudolf's left hand, a finger of his right hand and half of one foot.

Because the hypsometer had not worked, Annie could only estimate Huascarán's height. At the saddle she and her guides had measured the altitude at 20,000 feet (6,100 meters). Based on this figure, they estimated that the north and south peaks were at least 23,000 feet (7,000 meters), making Huascarán the highest mountain in Peru and the highest mountain ever scaled by a man or woman.

Fanny Bullock Workman, up to this time the world's highest woman climber, challenged Annie's estimate of Huascarán. Bullock Workman sent a team of scientists to Yungay to measure Huascarán by triangulation: This method uses trigonometry to measure height. Bullock Workman's team concluded that the north and south peaks were no more than 21,812 feet (6,648 meters) and 22,187 feet (6,763 meters) respectively.

Annie eventually conceded that Huascarán was "not so lofty" as she had hoped. Bullock Workman still held the world's altitude record for a woman climber, but Annie had succeeded in climbing a mountain that no man or woman had ever climbed. Annie continued climbing until she was eighty-two years old.

Annie Smith Peck wearing her mountain-climbing gear

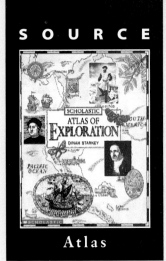

FROM

ATLAS OF
EXPLORATION

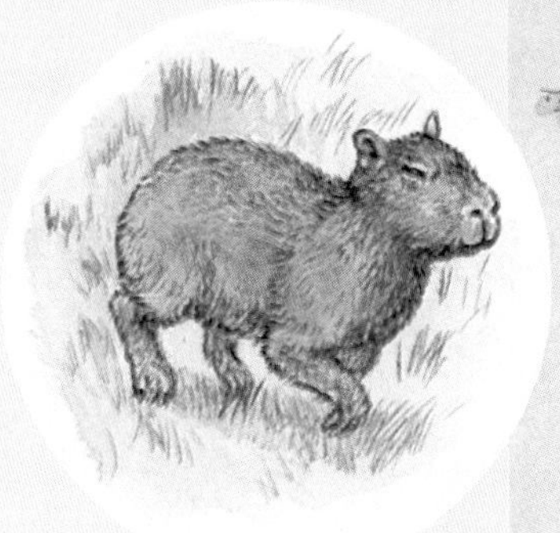

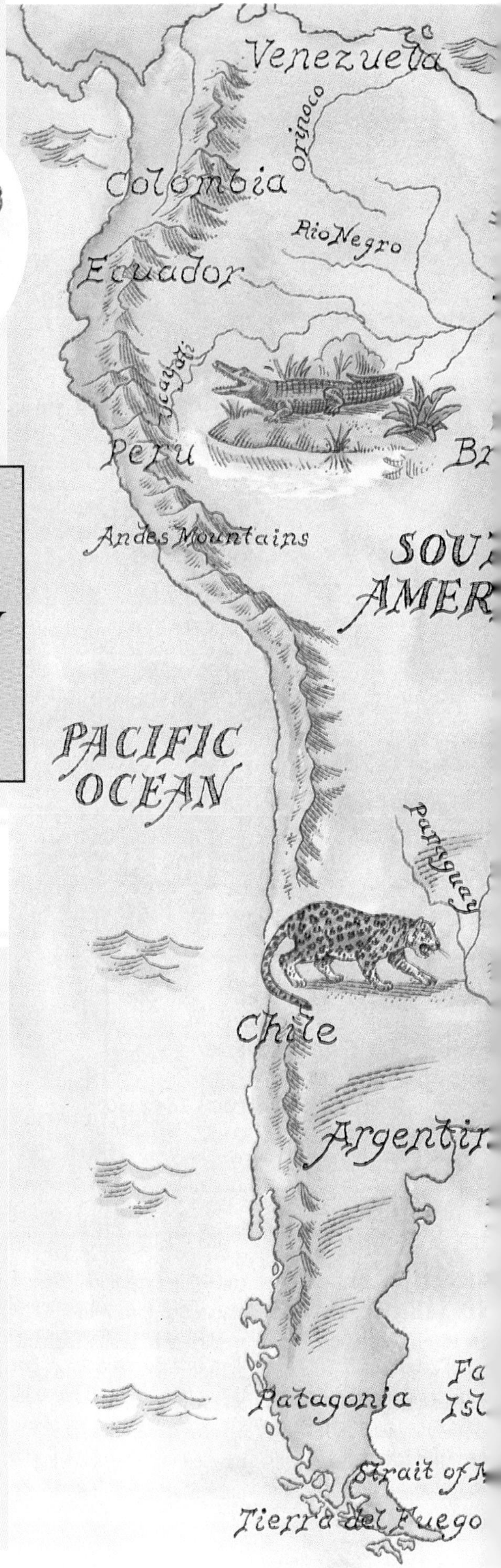

By Dinah Starkey

EXPLORING
SOUTH AMERICA

The explorers who traveled down the Amazon were the first Europeans to enter the rainforests. For the most part, they journeyed by raft or canoe. It was an environment unlike anything they had ever seen.

Everywhere the explorers looked, there were strange, new things. The waters of the Amazon were full of life. There were alligators sixteen feet long, large swimming rodents called capybara, water snakes, and turtles. In some places there were piranha fish, which could strip a man's arm to the bone in ten minutes, and shoals of stingrays. Electric eels swam in the shallows.

Venezuela

Colombia

Orinoco

Rio Negro

Ecuador

Ucayali

Peru

Andes Mountains

SOU
AMER

Br

PACIFIC
OCEAN

Paraguay

Chile

Argentir

Patagonia

Fa
Isl

Strait of

Tierra del Fuego

ATLANTIC OCEAN

What the explorers brought back
The explorers of South America brought back:

RUBBER

GOLD

PLATINUM

MAHOGANY

N

W E

S

0   300   600 m

THE PEOPLES OF SOUTH AMERICA

The explorers found many different groups of Native Americans living in the South American rainforest. They all lived primarily by farming, growing crops such as cassava, beans, corn, squash, and sweet potatoes. Cassava was their most important crop. Its roots contain poison, which the native people removed by grating and squeezing the roots. They ground the remains into meal for making bread.

The native people knew the rainforest very well. They knew all about the plants: which ones were poisonous and which could be used as food and medicine. They were skillful hunters, killing fish, animals, and birds of the rainforest for food. Their weapons included spears, bows and arrows, blowguns, nets, hooks, and potions for stunning fish.

The tribes of South America had customs, religions, and traditions that were very different from those Europeans were used to. Depending on the tribe, some people covered their bodies with painted designs and wore ornate jewelry. Others made holes in their cheeks with sharp pieces of bone or tattooed themselves all over. Children of the Arua tribe had their earlobes stretched by weights to appear more beautiful. One tribe, the Amazons, was led by women.

ALEXANDER VON HUMBOLDT This German explorer was rich enough to pay for his own expedition in 1799. He was eager to learn all he could about South America and traveled all over the continent, often at great risk. He explored the Orinoco River, climbed the high Andes Mountains, peered into the mouth of a live volcano, and got a shock from an electric eel. One of his discoveries was the Humboldt Current—a cold sea current off the coast of Peru. Humboldt

was interested in the peoples of South America. He saw that Europeans often treated them badly. When he returned home, he worked hard to tell others about this and to help bring about change.

EXPLORERS OF THE NORTH POLE

At the top of the world lies the coldest ocean on Earth. It is the Arctic Ocean, where the water freezes into solid ice that can trap a ship forever.

For thousands of years people have known about the Arctic Ocean and its dangers. The ancient Greeks had explored this area and they believed it marked the end of the Earth.

Europeans began to explore it a few years after Columbus, da Gama, and Magellan made their great journeys of discovery. The captains of these European expeditions were looking for a northern passage to the Spice Islands. Spain and Portugal had claimed the two best routes by going south. Other nations hoped to find a different way by going far north.

FRIDTJOF NANSEN

Nansen was a Norwegian, born in 1861. He knew that the waters of the Arctic, though frozen, moved very slowly. He believed that if he built a boat strong enough to withstand the ice, he could drift in it

towards the North Pole. The attempt took three years. Although Nansen didn't reach the Pole, his journey taught other explorers a great deal about living in the Arctic.

ROBERT PEARY

In 1909 two men took part in a race to reach the North Pole. Robert Peary and Dr. Frederick Cook were both Americans. Peary planned his expedition very carefully. He took 133 dogs and 12 sleds and used Inuit (Eskimo) guides. On April 6, 1909, Peary reached the North Pole with Matthew Henson and four Inuit. Dr. Cook later claimed he had reached the Pole before Peary, but people now believe that Cook was mistaken.

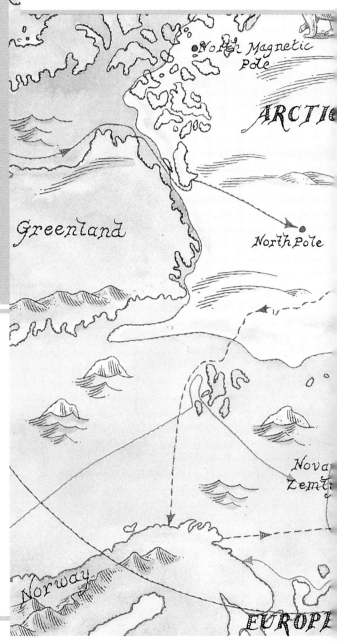

KEY TO MAP
Barents
Bering
Nansen
Peary

Bering Strait

Siberia

Arctic Circle

ASIA

KEY DATES

- **1596** Barents wintered in the Arctic
- **1724** Bering left for eastern Asia
- **1893-6** Nansen sailed across the Arctic
- **1909** Peary reached the North Pole

VITUS BERING

Bering served in the Russian Navy. In 1724 Peter the Great sent him to find out whether Asia was joined to North America. Bering discovered that the two continents were separated by a strait (narrow channel). This body of water is now named the Bering Strait.

WILLEM BARENTS

The Dutch sent Willem Barents to explore the areas to the north and east of Norway, where they believed they might find a northeast passage to the Pacific Ocean.

In 1596 Barents was sailing off the coast of Novaya Zemlya in the Arctic Ocean when the sea began to freeze. Winter was beginning and the crew was trapped.

Ice formed around the ship, cracking its timbers and forcing it up out of the water. The sailors walked across the ice until they got to shore, carrying wood from the ship with them. They built a hut out of the wood and they stayed there all through the winter, on a shore that they named "Ice Haven." It was so cold that the sheets froze on their beds. The men survived the winter by hunting animals and living off the supplies from the ship.

In 1871, nearly 300 years later, another expedition found the hut, just as Barents and his men had left it. The cooking pots and weapons, the ship's clock, and even the cabin boy's boots, were still there, preserved by the cold.

PEOPLE OF THE ARCTIC

The Inuit were expert at surviving in the extreme cold. Their clothes were warmer and lighter than anything the explorers could make. They dressed in jackets and pants of sealskin. Their boots were stuffed with moss. In winter they traveled by dogsled and, when the thaw came, they used kayaks—canoes made of whale bone and hide.

EXPLORERS OF THE SOUTH POLE

The explorers who tried to reach the South Pole faced terrible dangers. Ships sailing around Antarctica met icebergs big enough to sink them. To the south, the Ross Ice Shelf, a vast cliff of ice, bars the way to the Antarctic continent. The land at the South Pole is a mixture of snowfields and mountain peaks. Hidden under the snow there are crevasses—deep cracks in the ice that can swallow up a sled or a team of dogs. Hunger, fatigue, cold, and frostbite are all enemies of travelers in the Antarctic.

TWO POLES

There are two South Poles. One is the South Magnetic Pole. This is the point that draws the needle of the compass. The other is the geographic South Pole. This is in the exact center of the Arctic Circle and is the point that Scott and Amundsen were trying to reach. There are two North Poles also.

JAMES CLARK ROSS

An officer in the British navy, James Clark Ross was the first man to discover the North Magnetic Pole between 1829 and 1833.

He also explored Antarctica. In 1841 he took two strong ships, the *Erebus* and the *Terror*, south through pack-ice and past live volcanoes until they came to a great wall of ice. This is now called the Ross Ice Shelf.

SOUTH AMERICA

ATLANTIC OCEAN

Weddell Sea

Ronne Ice Shelf

ANTARCTIC

South Pole

Ross Sea

Bay of Whales

Ross Ice Shelf

McMurdo Sound

South Magnetic

PACIFIC OCEAN

Antarctic Circle

RACE FOR THE SOUTH POLE

In 1911 two expeditions set out to reach the South Pole. One was British: Captain Robert Scott sailed from London towards Antarctica in the *Terra Nova*. He took a large team of scientists with him, including a film camera operator. When he reached Melbourne, Australia, Scott found a telegram waiting for him. It was from Roald Amundsen, a Norwegian explorer, who planned to race him to the Pole. Amundsen's team started the journey from his base in the Bay of Whales on October 20, 1911. They traveled quickly because they had little to carry. On December 14, 1911, they reached the South Pole, where they raised the Norwegian flag and put up a tent. Inside, they left letters for Scott. Then they returned to their ship and sailed safely home.

Scott left from his base at McMurdo Sound on November 1, 1911, but the ponies that he planned to use in the final stretch to the Pole died in the extreme cold. Scott's men had to help pull the sleds themselves because Scott had not brought enough dogs. The expedition soon ran into more trouble. The men grew very tired and Scott had to send back the sleds one after another, until there was only one left. On January 18, 1912, Scott and four teammates reached the South Pole. There they found the Norwegian flag, so they knew that Amundsen had beaten them to it. They started to make their way back to base, but they were tired and suffering badly from frostbite. Not one of them reached the base camp. All five men died on the way.

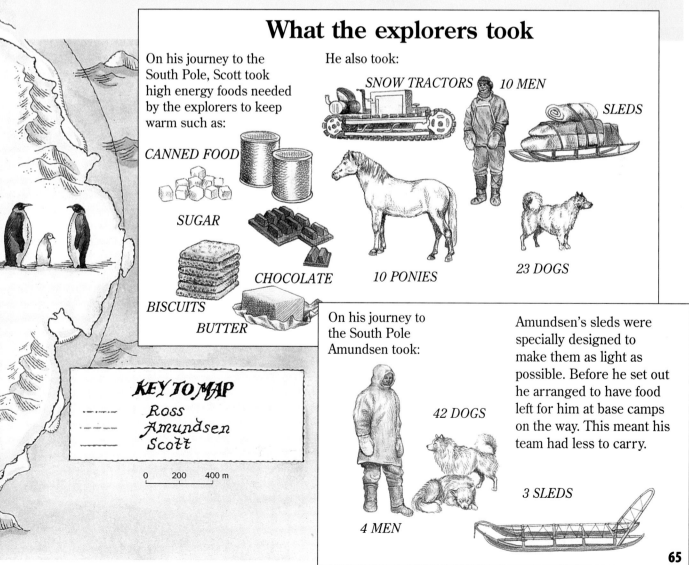

What the explorers took

On his journey to the South Pole, Scott took high energy foods needed by the explorers to keep warm such as:

CANNED FOOD

SUGAR

CHOCOLATE

BISCUITS

BUTTER

He also took:

SNOW TRACTORS 10 MEN

SLEDS

10 PONIES

23 DOGS

KEY TO MAP
Ross
Amundsen
Scott

0   200   400 m

On his journey to the South Pole Amundsen took:

42 DOGS

4 MEN

Amundsen's sleds were specially designed to make them as light as possible. Before he set out he arranged to have food left for him at base camps on the way. This meant his team had less to carry.

3 SLEDS

THE FUTURE OF EXPLORATION

We have now explored almost all of the Earth's land surface. Because of this, modern-day exploration is quite different from what it was in previous centuries. Gone are the days when courageous men and women set out for unexplored territories, not knowing whether they would survive the hazards of unknown peoples, strange diseases, or wild animals. Modern explorers still have uncharted territories on Earth to explore such as the densest parts of the rainforest, the Antarctic regions, and the oceans. Most explorers of the 20th century are scientists and conservationists, eager to learn about the Earth and its climate, the balance that exists between all of the Earth's living things and ways to preserve and protect this balance.

THE ANTARCTIC
Antarctica was the last land surface on Earth to be fully explored when, in 1958, an expedition crossed the continent for the first time. Large areas of this freezing continent are still not known to us in any detail, but this is gradually changing since many international scientific stations are now based there. Scientists study the layers of ice, which show the composition of the snow that has fallen over the last 160,000 years. From this they can find out about long-term changes in Earth's climate and atmosphere.

THE RAINFORESTS

The tropical rainforests of Africa and South America contain millions of different animal and plant species, most of which have not been identified or named. In the more remote areas, there is still a lot of scientific exploration that can be done, especially with regard to the "canopy" of the rainforest (this is the name given to the mass of foliage high up in the trees).

Exploration has damaged the rainforests. It has led to people living outside the area destroying the rainforest for their own profit by lumbering, mining, and cattle-grazing. Only now are scientists going there to study the plants and animals of the rainforest in an effort to reverse the damage that has been caused.

STILL UNEXPLORED

Other areas of the Earth that have been only partly explored include high mountain areas, underground rivers and caves (left), the ocean bed, and desert areas. Projects continue to bring to light new facts on the Earth's make-up and to monitor the changes that are taking place, such as the expansion of the desert regions.

THE SKY IS THE LIMIT

As long as there have been places to explore, there have been people willing to take the risks and challenges involved in exploration. The greatest challenge in the 21st century for these men and women will be the continued exploration of space. Space travel has advanced in leaps and bounds, and it is possible that in the future someone will step on to the planet Mars. The wonder and vastness of space beckons to all those who consider themselves explorers.

From

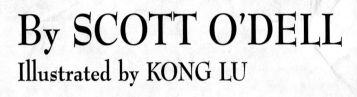

BLACK STAR, BRIGHT DAWN

By SCOTT O'DELL
Illustrated by KONG LU

*Eighteen-year-old Bright Dawn can't believe
she's competing in the famous Iditarod
dog sled race. The trail is one thousand miles
long between Anchorage and Nome, Alaska,
with many dangers along the route. With
the help of Black Star, her favorite sled dog,
and Oteg, a kind old man she meets at the
starting line, Bright Dawn races toward
Iditarod, a major stop along the trail.*

T HE TRAIL through
Ptarmigan was steep. The new sled
flew like a frightened bird. At the
bottom of the pass, just as I skimmed
out of a grove of spruce trees, I saw
something strange on the trail.

Snow was falling, and at first I thought it was a pile of rocks covered by brush. As I drew closer, the rocks turned into trees, then into a shaggy beast. I thought it was a caribou. Then I saw the spreading horns and the long lumpy nose. It was a moose, a bull moose, big and red-eyed.

Moose are always dangerous. They are big and bad-tempered. Oteg was far behind, and if I waited for him to come and help me I would lose all the time I had gained.

I did not dare to challenge the beast. Once when I was with my father we met a young bull near Blue Goose Village. It was standing in the middle of the trail, swinging its head back and forth.

"It does not wish to move," Bartok said.

"I don't blame him," I said. "The trail is easier to walk on than deep snow."

"And what's more, it is not going to move. It weighs most of seven hundred pounds, so we are not going to make him move."

"We can try."

"Remember old Ekaluk? He tried one time and lost three of his dogs and came close to losing his life. I have my gun, but since my eyes went bad I am a poor shot. If I only wound the beast, it will come at us."

He unhitched Black Star and the rest of the team. He turned the sled around, hitched up the dogs again, and we went back, nearly out of sight, and waited. We waited for most of an hour, until the beast decided to move away.

69

What had happened to Ekaluk I did not want to happen to me. Oteg had good advice about passing dog teams but not about passing a moose. I stepped down on the brake and shouted "Whoa" to Black Star. When the team came to a halt, I was so close to the animal I could hear it breathing. Its head was lowered and it stared at me with its yellow eyes.

Quietly I put on my snowshoes. I made a half circle around the moose, leaving a trail in the snow that was deep enough to run on. The dogs were barking, straining at their leashes in a frenzy to get at the beast. They did not budge when I yelled "Go!" I had to crack the long, black whip over their heads before they would take the trail. They barked until the moose was out of sight behind us.

It stopped snowing and a weak sun came out, but the wind still blew hard from the north. I passed two teams camped beside the trail. Close to dusk I came upon a third team. The driver was pulled up behind some trees, feeding his dogs.

He raised a hand and shouted, "Watch for moose. Two big ones just trotted by." He pointed down the trail to Rohn. "I'd wait, young lady. You can get into trouble," he shouted.

"I just passed one," I shouted back, thinking that he was not warning me but trying to slow me down.

But in a short time, as the trail climbed a hill and went down again over a bridge and frozen stream, I saw the moose, the ones the driver had warned me about. There were two of them, as he had said, a bull and a cow. The bull was big. Each of my dogs weighed over seventy pounds. The bull looked bigger than all of them put together.

When she heard the dogs bark, the cow took to the stream and disappeared. But the bull stood sideways on the bridge and did not move. I pulled up the team as soon as I was sure that he meant to stay there.

Off to the right of the bridge were patches of earth and rocks where the wind had swept the snow clean. I shouted "Gee!" for right turns, then "Haw!" for left turns, and Black Star picked his way through the clean patches.

When we were safely on the trail again I glanced back at the bull. He had moved from the bridge. He was slowly trotting after us, swinging his head from side to side. I cracked the whip and the team leaped forward. But as we picked up speed, the bull did not stop, and I saw that he was chasing us.

In a long run my dogs could outdistance him—they can cover close to twenty miles in an hour—but in a short run moose could run much faster. They run at a gallop, thrusting their thin legs ahead of their bodies, two powerful legs at a time.

I was scared. I jumped off the sled to make it easier for the dogs. The moose rushed up and ran beside me. For a moment I thought he was showing off, playing some sort of a wild game. Then he ran past me and galloped along the line of dogs, brushing them off the trail with his broad antlers.

He galloped on and disappeared over the brow of the hill. My dogs were barking, trying to get out of their harness to chase him, so I waited for a while to calm them down and let the bull gallop out of sight.

But when we started up again and came to the brow of the hill, he was waiting. He stood in the middle of the trail, his long, queer-shaped nose raised to the wind and his yellow eyes fixed on us.

We were in a draw with boulders on both sides of the trail. There was no way to get around the beast, but room to turn back. I made the turn and waited beyond the hill for Oteg, for one of the drivers, for help to come.

No sooner had I calmed the dogs again than the bull appeared on the brow of the hill.

He stood for a moment looking down at us, pawing the snow. With one sweep of his antlers he could kill half the team. With his sharp hoofs he could injure the rest.

I did a desperate thing. As the bull started toward us, I ran down the towline, loosened the buckles, and freed all of the dogs. It was better that they run or hide, to save themselves as best they could, than to be caught tied to a towline.

Black Star raised his head, growled, and moved slowly up the rise to meet the bull. The rest of the dogs followed. The sled was small protection, yet I stood behind it. Not long before I had felt the biting wind. I felt it no longer.

Black Star circled the bull once, twice, three times, drawing closer each time. On the last circle the beast caught him a glancing blow with one of its back hoofs and sent him sprawling.

Black Star shook the snow out of his eyes, got up, and stalked the bull again. Now all of my dogs sent up chilling howls and joined him.

The bull snorted, made sounds like far-off thunder, and slashed out with his sharp hoofs. He moved round and round. He tried to face all the dogs at once but failed. Then he made a dash for Sky and gave her a slashing blow with both of his front hoofs.

I took off my parka, ran up the trail, and waved it frantically—a foolish thing to do, yet it saved us. The moose forgot he was surrounded by growling dogs.

For a moment his blazing eyes examined me and the parka. In that brief time, Black Star sunk his teeth into the beast's throat. In a flash the other dogs were on him.

The moose fell to his knees and rolled over. He tried to shed the dogs, but they clung to him until he lay still.

I wrapped Sky in my heavy parka and laid her on the sled. She was scarcely breathing. I rounded up the dogs and fastened them to the towline and started for Rohn. It was getting dark. The trail was hard to see, but I turned on my headlamp and went fast.

IT WAS PAST THREE in the morning when I came to Rohn. A north wind was blowing. I anchored the sled and took Sky in my arms. She seemed better. But when I got her to the cabin—this was all of Rohn, a cabin beside the trail—and the veterinarian looked at her, he said that she had three broken ribs. He gave her something and she went to sleep.

Oteg came in more than an hour after I did. He had lost the trail out of Ptarmigan and ended up in a swamp.

"How many teams did you pass?" he asked.

"Four."

He clapped his hands. "Pass four today. I stay close. No more swamps. We push the leaders, not too fast, not too slow. To the others we give serious thoughts. And all the time we keep the dogs strong. Dogs win the races."

I told him about the moose.

"They are worse than blizzards," he said. "And the trails you cannot find in the snow. Holes in the ice and swamps. Moose are the worst. But today you need not worry about them. I will speak to my friend, the Raven."

A big fire was going in the cabin. He shouldered his way through the crowd of mushers, warmed his hands at the fire, and went outside. When he came back, he said that he had spoken a few words to Raven.

The stars were dim and there was a small moon. I cooked food for the team, staked it out away from the other teams, and changed the boots on all the dogs that needed them. Then I crawled into the sleeping bag, slept until dawn, and went to see about my injured dog.

She was awake but did not want the fish I brought her or any of the meat the plane had dropped or the rice and blueberry cakes I had stored away for myself.

"Do you want to *go?*" I said in the voice I used on the trail.

She cocked her ears. She looked up at me for a moment, then closed her eyes.

The morning had dawned clear and cold. I could hear the drivers talking to their dogs. The first teams were leaving. Oteg came in and wanted to know if I was ready.

"Twelve teams have gone," he said. "I am hitched. But still you moon over the dog." He was angry.

I said nothing and went out and told the marshal that I wanted to send my dog back to Anchorage. He said a plane was due.

"When?" I asked.

"In an hour, depending on the wind."

Oteg had followed me. He guessed that I meant to wait and put my dog on the plane.

"You do not win races this way," he said. "Maybe the plane comes in an hour. Maybe in two hours. Maybe tomorrow. Who knows?"

The marshal said, "The veterinarian will take care of your dog. And I'll see that she gets on the plane."

I thanked him and said I would wait for the plane. He gave me a quick glance and shook his head. Silently, Oteg left the cabin. I heard him shouting at his dogs, the crack of his whip, and the squeal of the runners.

The plane landed in less than an hour. I wrapped Sky in a blanket, Mr. McCall gave her a pill, and I put her on the plane.

"Will they take care of Sky when she gets to Anchorage?" I asked him.

"She'll have a better time than pulling a sled."

Mr. McCall did not know that she would rather pull a sled than eat.

I got the rest of the team ready and we left before noon. The sky was gray, but it had stopped snowing. I caught up with Oteg. He pulled off the trail so I could pass. He had gotten over his anger and shouted more advice. I did not listen. He had taught me many things about the race. But it was Oteg who was racing in the Iditarod, not me.

I remembered my father's words. He said, "Do not depend on other people, on me, on your teachers in school, on anybody. Listen and think about what you hear, but depend upon yourself." From now on I would try not to depend upon Oteg so much.

It seemed strange driving the team without Sky. The team missed her, too. She sang a lot even when we were going uphill and the snow was deep.

The afternoon turned cold. Sharp pebbles covered the trail. They were hard on the dogs' feet. I stopped twice to feed them bits of frozen meat and change their boots.

At dusk I came to the Farewell Burn. Oteg had told me about the Farewell Burn. It was thousands of acres that a fire had swept through. Stumps of burned trees rose everywhere along the trail. A thin sheet of snow covered them like shrouds. In the dim light they looked like rows of ghostly heads.

Oteg had warned me to go slow through the Burn, to watch closely for stumps. Instead, now that I was running the race in my own way, I drove faster than I should have. I hit one of the stumps and broke off pieces of both of the runners. I drove slower after that and Oteg passed me.

I got to Nikolai, the next checkpoint, at two in the morning, almost an hour after he did. It was blowing again. The wind turned into a blizzard. The thermometer fell way below zero. You could not see beyond your feet. A "freeze" was called, and not a team stirred that day.

During this time Oteg built another igloo. Or, rather, we built it together. This time, at his prompting, I stood inside. He handed me the blocks of snow and I put them down in a circle and slanted the edges to make the dome. It was not so good as the igloo we had made at Rainy Pass, but it kept out the fierce wind.

The "freeze" helped. I could not race on broken runners. New ones were not to be found in Nikolai, but Oteg poked through his bundles and found two lengths of spruce, which he fitted to the runners and bound with caribou sinew.

"I will now make the runners smooth, both of them," he said. "Now you will fly!"

He took out a blob of frozen mud and heated it over the lamp. When it was soft, he went outside and smeared it over the runners and let it freeze again. With his knife he trimmed the mud smooth. Last, he filled his mouth with water and let it warm. Then he moved up and down the overturned sled with a piece of wet deerskin, spraying and wiping the runners. They froze in a second.

"Try it now," he said.

I put my hand on the sled and it moved easily.

"Try one finger."

I touched a finger to the sled. It glided away.

"Aiee, aiee," he crowed. "When we leave Nikolai we will go a little faster than before. We will pass some teams this time."

I nodded and thanked him for saving the sled.

Just before dawn, at a lull in the screaming wind, I heard the wolf sounds again, the sounds I had heard at Skwentna.

I went outside. All of the dogs except Black Star were buried in the snow. He was on his feet, sniffing the air. His head was turned toward a grove of trees. Beyond the trees, through the driving ice and snow, I made out the white wolf. He was standing with his pack, bunched

together. They were watching us and not making a sound.

Black Star was chained to the towline. I untied the chain, led him into the igloo, and set the snow blocks in place. For a short time I dozed and woke to find him clawing at the doorway. I sat up and listened.

The wolves had come closer. They seemed to be just outside the igloo, among the sleeping dogs.

Oteg crawled out of his bag. He put a chunk of seal oil in the lamp and set water to boil for his black tea.

"The wolves are outside," I said.

"I have heard them," Oteg said. "They are looking for food. They'll find none and go away."

"It's the same wolf pack I saw before. The leader is white. He's the one I saw at Skwentna. He's not just looking for food."

"You saw the white one?"

"This morning."

Oteg sighed. "It's Raven again. I'll attend to him after a while."

He put on his boots. He poured himself a mug of tea. He drank it and poured more. Then he got into his big parka and left the igloo. He was gone for a long time. I went outside, holding Black Star on his chain. Day was breaking.

Oteg stood with his mug of tea, looking at the sky. "It's very good," he said.

The sky was pink in the east. Bands of lavender shifted back and forth overhead, faded out, and returned in shades of orange and yellow.

"Where are the wolves?" I asked him.

He had forgotten about the wolves. He sipped his tea and gazed at the beautiful sky.

"The wolves," I said. "What happened to them?"

He drank his tea and kept admiring the sky.

WE LEFT Nikolai the next morning when the sun came up and got to McGrath at dusk. We camped there past midnight, looked after the dogs, slept some, and started off for Tokotna and Ophir and Iditarod.

Oteg said, "The driver who gets to Iditarod first wins two thousand dollars in silver money. That is a good prize, two thousand dollars. But I cannot win. I am too far back. Let the others scramble and wear out their dogs, is what I think. What do you think?"

It was the only time he had ever asked my opinion about anything.

"The new sled flies. The dogs are fine. Two thousand dollars is a lot of money, Mr. Oteg. I am going to try for it."

"Well…" He was disappointed, but he gave me a thin smile and wished me luck.

The dogs strained at their traces. They started off with a mighty rush. The runners sang. It was a dark night. Not a star showed.

Far in the west a pale moon went down. I passed six teams on the way to Tokotna, on the way to Ophir, eight teams. Now I was running ninth.

Beyond Ophir, the mushers ahead of me had stopped at a checkpoint called Don's Cabin. Warm lights shone through the window and I heard loud voices and laughter. It was very cold outside, but as soon as I checked in, I climbed back on the sled and headed down the trail for Iditarod.

We all had left Ophir according to the times we got there, also our places in the race. At every checkpoint, these staggered starts were used. In this way every musher could keep the advantage he or she had earned.

The country beyond Don's Cabin looked wild and forsaken. Scattered trees were ragged and bent over by the fierce winds. It was very cold. My feet stuck to the runners. They felt as if they belonged to somebody else.

I drove the team faster than I ever had before. At times we were running at fifteen miles an hour. The dogs opened their jaws and scooped up snow as they ran. I stopped and fed them snacks often enough to keep them happy.

No one was ahead of me. Not one of the eight drivers I had left at Don's Cabin had overtaken me. Yet I had no idea how much time I had gained on them or where I stood now in the race. Surely I was close to second or third.

Iditarod is a ghost town, just a few shacks left over from the gold rush, when ten thousand people lived there. As I drove in and put on the brakes, sending up a shower of snow, a marshal came out to greet me. He looked at his watch, put down figures in a book, and talked to people.

There was a long wait. Then a man came out and said, "Congratulations. You are the first driver to reach Iditarod. You are the winner of two thousand dollars."

I couldn't be the winner, but here I was. I felt giddy in the head. I had never earned more than fifty dollars making and selling mukluks. I tried to say a little speech. All I could say was, "Thank you."

SOURCE
ACTION
Magazine

AWARD WINNING Magazine

The Last Great Race

1,000 Miles Across Alaska by Dogsled

SUSAN BUTCHER stands in the middle of a frozen, snow-covered lake. For six days, she has been racing her team of sled dogs. They have crossed icy rivers and snowy mountains. It's so cold, Susan keeps stopping to wipe the dogs' eyes. Otherwise, their eyes will freeze closed.

Susan is exhausted. She's slept two hours each night since the race began. She wants to stop and rest. But another racer is close behind. She can't waste a minute.

"Go ahead!" she calls out to the lead dogs. All 16 dogs jump to their feet. They take off. Susan rides on the back of the sled, her feet on the runners. "Haw!" she yells, giving the signal to turn left. The team turns. Then they speed ahead.

The race Susan is trying to win is the Iditarod (i-DIT-a-rod). It has been called "The Last Great Race." It's held every March in Alaska. The trail of the race is 1,049 miles long. And it takes as long as 28 days to finish.

The racers, called "mushers," run their dogs day and night. They stop only to feed and rest the dogs. The risks are big. The mushers can get frostbite when the temperature drops to 60 degrees below zero. They can get caught in 80-mile-an-hour winds. And a blizzard can make it impossible to see.

The first place winner of the Iditarod gets $50,000. But the real excitement of the race is the physical and mental challenge. "It's a true endurance test," says Susan. "It takes all you've got in skill and character."

Susan has been racing in the Iditarod for over a decade. When Susan was 20, she moved to Alaska. She started breeding Alaskan husky dogs. Huskies are descended from old-time Indian and Eskimo dogs. They have thick coats and tough paws. That makes them perfect for sled racing.

Susan uses 16 dogs for a race. Each dog has its own personality. She puts them in pairs where they will work best. She picks the lead dogs for their intelligence and leadership. They must be able to find the trail if she falls asleep by accident.

In September, Susan starts training the dogs. At first, they run on bare ground, pulling a cart with wheels. Later, when the first snow falls, they use a sled. Soon, they are running 60 miles a day.

It's not only the dogs who have to get in shape. Mushers often run behind the sled during the race. To stay strong, they run, hike, or lift weights. Many also prepare for the race by sleeping less and less each night. By the time the race starts, they're used to getting by with very little sleep.

The first week in March, the race begins. As many as 60 mushers and 1,000 dogs are there. Susan's dogs are eager to run. Ten people have to hold them at the starting line until the signal is given.

Once the race starts, Susan races for four hours. Then she takes a four-hour break. She continues that way night and day.

During the breaks, the dogs sleep. But Susan works hard. She cooks food for the dogs. She fixes the sled. If she's lucky, she gets a 15-minute nap. Then, it's back to the trail.

Last year, Susan ran a hard race. She got so tired, she started to hallucinate. But she didn't stop. Finally, after almost 12 days of racing, Susan saw her dream come true. She and her dogs won the Iditarod. They did it in only 11 days, 15 hours, and 6 minutes—a world record.

"The toughness of this race makes winning it incredible," said Susan afterwards. "It's knowing you have what it takes to win. This race is the ultimate experience of my life."

How to
Compile an Equipment Checklist

What supplies should someone take on a hike in the woods, a canoe trip, or a visit to a new city? Taking the right equipment can mean the difference between a successful trip and a trip full of problems. That's why it's important to put together an equipment checklist before going to a new place.

What is an equipment checklist? An equipment checklist is a list of all the things needed for a particular trip. An equipment list helps a person remember all the items that will make the trip comfortable and safe.

EQUIPMENT CHECKLIST

Mt. Rainier Hiking Expedition

Essential Items

The following items need to be carried as close to the exact specifications as is possible, in order to minimize the weight you'll be carrying with you. Buying a specific brand is not essential, as long as the particular product you choose maximizes efficiency and minimizes weight. Any brands that meet these specifications are acceptable.

- down sleeping bag rated to 10–15°F; two that might be appropriate are 20°F, 2 lb 5 oz for those who sleep warm, and a heavier version at 5°F, 3 lb 2 oz for those who sleep cold. We strongly recommend getting a compression stuff sack to save room.
- small flashlight or head lamp (5 oz with 2 AA batteries)
- warm, water-resistant thermal ski jacket weighing 1 lb 6 oz
- warm, water-resistant thermal ski pants weighing 1 lb 2 oz
- waterproof rain slicker
- one cotton t-shirt
- one wool or flannel long-sleeve shirt
- one pair of lightweight cotton trousers
- two pairs thin liner socks made of polypropylene or silk
- one pair heavy Norwegian rag-wool outer socks
- lightweight hiking boots or well-broken-in leather hiking boots
- warm gloves
- duckbill baseball cap or Alpine hat
- one-liter water bottle
- personal medications, including prescription drugs, lip balm, lotion
- toiletries, all in compact, lightweight varieties (brush, tooth-paste, soap)
- medium-sized pack with rain cover to contain all of the above

● The destination is given.

● Necessary equipment is listed.

Items on the checklist include appropriate clothing.

● Important personal items are included.

1 Plan a Trip

Here's the chance to plan the trip of your dreams. Get together with some classmates and choose a place you would all like to visit. It can be a specific place, such as Mt. Everest, or it can be a type of trip, such as a cruise. Look at a globe or flip through an atlas if you need ideas. Discuss each place or type of trip that is suggested. Then agree on the one place you'd all like to go. Decide how long you'd like to stay there, what you will do and see, what the weather might be like, and what items you will need to have a good trip.

TOOLS

- atlas or globe
- travel brochures and magazines
- paper and pencil
- books about the place

2 Research and Record

Create a list of things you think you'd like to bring on your trip and things you will need—from maps to video games. To figure out what you need, research your place. Look in an atlas or an encyclopedia to find out more about where you're going. It's also a good idea to find out about the climate and the terrain of the place. After you've researched the location, take a sheet of paper and record everyone's ideas about what to bring. Will you need special clothing? money? a map? Write about why each item is important. What problems could it solve? How would it be useful?

3 Evaluate

Here's the catch—there's not enough room to bring everything on your list. Review all the items. Which are absolutely necessary? Why? Circle those items on your list. Keep in mind that you will be carrying your own gear, so don't bring anything unnecessary—and keep it light.

Tip Even if your decision about what to bring seems right to you, listen to others in your group, and always keep an open mind. You may have forgotten something that you will need.

4 Create and Present

Create your checklist by writing general information about the trip at the top of a sheet of paper. Then list the equipment you've decided on. After you're done, present your checklist to your group and explain why you need the items you've chosen.

If You Are Using a Computer . . .

Write notes about your trip in the Journal format on the computer. When you create your list, use interesting fonts and clip art to illustrate the items on your list.

THINK

In what other situations might an equipment checklist be helpful?

Cesar Rivera
Emergency Worker ▶

Knowledge and skills help people survive in new environments.

Tools of Survival

Read about a boy who must figure out how to survive in the wild after a plane crash.

Explore a book of wilderness survival tips. Read a poem about staying alive in the wilderness.

PROJECT

Create a survival guide of important information.

The Desert Island Survival Guide

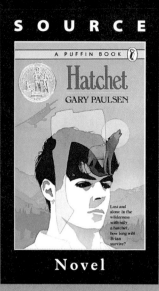

FROM HATCHET

BY GARY PAULSEN

ILLUSTRATED BY WAYNE McLOUGHLIN

Thirteen-year-old Brian Robeson is flying in a single-engine plane to visit his father in the Canadian wilderness. But when the pilot suffers a massive heart attack and dies, Brian crash lands the plane in a lake. Left with only the clothes he is wearing and a hatchet he received from his mother as a parting gift, Brian has spent weeks alone in the wilderness.

IN THE MORNING he rolled out before true light. In the gray dawn he built up the fire and found more wood for the day, feeling almost chipper because his ribs were much better now. With camp ready for the day he looked to the lake. Part of him half-expected the plane tail to be gone, sunk back into the depths, but he saw that it was still there, didn't seem to have moved at all.

He looked down at his feet and saw that there were some fish in his fish pen looking for the tiny bits of bait still left from before the wind came. He fought impatience to get on the plane project and remembered sense, remembered what he had learned. First food, because food made strength; first food, then thought, then action. There were fish at hand here, and he might not be able to get anything from the plane. That was all a dream.

The fish were real and his stomach, even his new shrunken stomach, was sending signals that it was savagely empty.

He made a fish spear with two points, not peeling the bark all the way back but just working on the pointed end. It took him an hour or so and all the time he worked he sat looking at the tail of the plane sticking up in the air, his hands working on the spear, his mind working on the problem of the plane.

When the spear was done, although still crude, he jammed a wedge between the points to spread them apart and went to the fish pond. There were not clouds of fish, but at least ten, and he picked one of the larger ones, a round fish almost six inches long, and put the spear point in the water, held it, then thrust with a flicking motion of his wrist when the fish was just above the point.

The fish was pinned neatly and he took two more with the same ease, then carried all three back up to the fire. He had a fish board now, a piece of wood he had flattened with the hatchet, that leaned up by the fire for cooking fish so he didn't have to hold a stick all the time. He put the three fish on the board, pushed sharpened pegs through their tails into cracks on the cooking board, and propped it next to the reddest part of the coals. In moments the fish were hissing and cooking with the heat and as soon as they were done, or when he could stand the smell no longer, he picked the steaming meat from under the loosened skin and ate it.

The fish did not fill him, did not even come close—fish meat was too light for that. But they gave him strength—he could feel it moving into his arms and legs—and he began to work on the plane project.

While making the spear he had decided that what he would have to do was make a raft and push-paddle the raft to the plane and tie it there for a working base. Somehow he would have to get into the tail, inside the plane—rip or cut his way in—and however he did it he would need an operating base of some kind. A raft.

Which, he found ruefully, was much easier said than done. There were plenty of logs around. The shore was littered with driftwood, new and old, tossed up and scattered by the tornado. And it was a simple matter to find four of them about the same length and pull them together.

Keeping them together was the problem. Without rope or crosspieces and nails the logs just rolled and separated. He tried wedging them together, crossing them over each other—nothing seemed to work. And he needed a stable platform to get the job done. It was becoming frustrating and he had a momentary loss of temper—as he would have done in the past, when he was the other person.

At that point he sat back on the beach and studied the problem again. Sense, he had

to use his sense. That's all it took to solve problems—just sense.

It came then. The logs he had selected were smooth and round and had no limbs. What he needed were logs with limbs sticking out, then he could cross the limbs of one log over the limbs of another and "weave" them together as he had done his wall, the food shelf cover, and the fish gate. He scanned the area above the beach and found four dry treetops that had been broken off by the storm. These had limbs and he dragged them down to his work area at the water's edge and fitted them together.

It took most of the day. The limbs were cluttered and stuck any which way and he would have to cut one to make another fit, then cut one from another log to come back to the first one, then still another from a third log would have to be pulled in.

But at last, in the late afternoon he was done and the raft—which he called Brushpile One for its looks—hung together even as he pulled it into the water off the beach. It floated well, if low in the water, and in the excitement he started for the plane. He could not stand on it, but would have to swim alongside.

He was out to chest depth when he realized he had no way to keep the raft at the plane. He needed some way to tie it in place so he could work from it.

And for a moment he was stymied. He had no rope, only the bowstring and the other cut shoestring in his tennis shoes— which were by now looking close to dead, his toes showing at the tops. Then he remembered his windbreaker and he found the tattered part he used for an arrow pouch. He tore it into narrow strips and tied them together to make a rope or tie-down about four feet long. It wasn't strong, he couldn't use it to pull a Tarzan and swing from a tree, but it should hold the raft to the plane.

Once more he slid the raft off the beach and out into the water until he was chest deep. He had left his tennis shoes in the shelter and when he felt the sand turn to mud between his toes he kicked off the bottom and began to swim.

Pushing the raft, he figured, was about like trying to push an aircraft carrier. All the branches that stuck down into the water dragged and pulled and the logs themselves fought any forward motion and he hadn't gone twenty feet when he realized that it was going to be much harder than he thought to get the raft to the plane. It barely moved and if he kept going this way he would just about reach the plane at dark. He decided to turn back again, spend the night and start early in the morning, and he pulled the raft once more onto the sand and wipe-scraped it dry with his hand.

Patience. He was better now but impatience still ground at him a bit so he sat at the edge of the fish pond with the new spear and took three more fish, cooked them up and ate them, which helped to pass the time until dark. He also dragged in more wood—endless wood—and then relaxed and watched the sun set over the trees in back of the ridge. West, he thought. I'm watching the sun set in the west. And that way was north where his father was, and that way east and that way south—and somewhere to the south and east his mother would be. The news would be on the television. He could visualize more easily his mother doing things than his father because he had never been to where his father lived now. He knew everything about how his mother lived. She would have the small television on the kitchen counter on and be watching the news and talking about how awful it was in South

chill. There it is again, he thought, that late summer chill to the air, the smell of fall. He went to sleep thinking a kind of reverse question. He did not know if he would ever get out of this, could not see how it might be, but if he did somehow get home and go back to living the way he had lived, would it be just the opposite? Would he be sitting watching television and suddenly think about the sunset up in back of the ridge and wonder how the color looked in the lake?

Sleep.

Africa or how cute the baby in the commercial looked. Talking and making sounds, cooking sounds.

He jerked his mind back to the lake. There was great beauty here—almost unbelievable beauty. The sun exploded the sky, just blew it up with the setting color, and that color came down into the water of the lake, lit the trees. Amazing beauty and he wished he could share it with somebody and say, "Look there, and over there, and see that..."

But even alone it was beautiful and he fed the fire to cut the night

IN THE MORNING the chill was more pronounced and he could see tiny wisps of vapor from his breath. He threw wood on the fire and blew until it flamed, then banked the flames to last and went down to the lake. Perhaps because the air was so cool the water felt warm as he waded in. He made sure the hatchet was still at his belt and the raft still held together, then set out pushing the raft and kick-swimming toward the tail of the plane.

As before, it was very hard going. Once an eddy of breeze came up against him and he seemed to be standing still and by the time he was close enough to the tail to see the rivets in the aluminum he had pushed and kicked for over two hours, was nearly exhausted and wished he had taken some time to get a fish or two and have breakfast. He was also wrinkled as a prune and ready for a break.

The tail looked much larger when he got next to it, with a major part of the vertical stabilizer showing and perhaps half of the elevators. Only a short piece of the top of the fuselage, the plane's body toward the tail, was out of the water, just a curve of aluminum, and at first he could see no place to tie the raft. But he pulled himself along the elevators to the end and there he found a gap that went in up by the hinges where he could feed his rope through.

With the raft secure he climbed on top of it and lay on his back for fifteen minutes, resting and letting the sun warm him.

The job, he thought, looked impossible. To have any chance of success he would have to be strong when he started.

Somehow he had to get inside the plane. All openings, even the small rear cargo hatch, were underwater so he couldn't get at them without diving and coming up inside the plane.

Where he would be trapped.

He shuddered at that thought and then remembered what was in the front of the plane, down in the bottom of the lake, still strapped in the seat, the body of the pilot. Sitting there in the water—Brian could see him, the big man with his hair waving in the current, his eyes open...

Stop, he thought. Stop now. Stop that thinking. He was nearly at the point of swimming back to shore and forgetting the whole thing. But the image of the survival pack kept him. If he could get it out of the plane, or if he could just get into it and pull something out. A candy bar.

Even that—just a candy bar. It would be worth it.

But how to get at the inside of the plane?

He rolled off the raft and pulled himself around the plane. No openings. Three times he put his face in the water and opened his eyes and looked down. The water was murky, but he could see perhaps six feet and there was no obvious way to get into the plane. He was blocked.

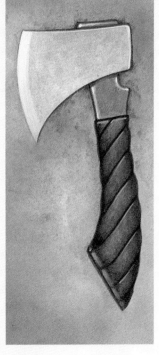

BRIAN WORKED around the tail of the plane two more times, pulling himself along on the stabilizer and the elevator, but there simply wasn't a way in.

Stupid, he thought. I was stupid to think I could just come out here and get inside the plane. Nothing is that easy. Not out here, not in this place. Nothing is easy.

He slammed his fist against the body of the plane and to his complete surprise the aluminum covering gave easily under his blow. He hit it again, and once more it bent and gave and he found that even when he didn't strike it but just pushed, it still moved. It was really, he thought, very thin aluminum skin over a kind of skeleton and if it gave that easily he might be able to force his way through...

The hatchet. He might be able to cut or hack with the hatchet. He reached to his belt and pulled the hatchet out, picked a place where the aluminum gave to his push and took an experimental swing at it.

The hatchet cut through the aluminum as if it were soft cheese. He couldn't believe it. Three more hacks and he had a triangular hole the size of his hand and he could see four cables that he guessed were the control cables going back to the tail and he hit the skin of the plane with a frenzied series of hacks to make a still larger opening and he was bending a piece of aluminum away from two aluminum braces of some kind when he dropped the hatchet.

It went straight down past his legs. He felt it bump his foot and then go on down, down into the water and for a second he couldn't understand that he had done it. For all this time, all the living and fighting, the hatchet had been everything—he had always worn it.

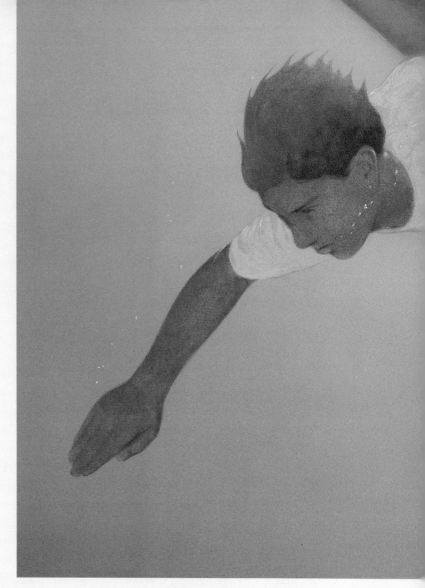

Without the hatchet he had nothing—no fire, no tools, no weapons—he was nothing. The hatchet was, had been him.

And he had dropped it.

"Arrrgghhh!" He yelled it, choked on it, a snarl-cry of rage at his own careless-ness. The hole in the plane was still too small to use for anything and now he didn't have a tool.

"That was the kind of thing I would have done before," he said to the lake, to the sky, to the trees. "When I came here—I would have done that. Not now. Not now..."

Yet he had and he hung on the raft for a moment and felt sorry for himself. For his own stupidity. But as before, the self-pity didn't help and he knew that he had only one course of action.

He had to get the hatchet back. He had to dive and get it back.

But how deep was it? In the deep end of the gym pool at school he had no trouble getting to the bottom and that was, he was pretty sure, about eleven feet.

Here it was impossible to know the exact depth. The front end of the plane, anchored by the weight of the engine, was obviously on the bottom but it came back up at an angle so the water wasn't as deep as the plane was long.

He pulled himself out of the water so his chest could expand, took two deep breaths and swiveled and dove, pulling his arms and kicking off the raft bottom with his feet.

His first thrust took him down a good eight feet but the visibility was only five feet beyond that

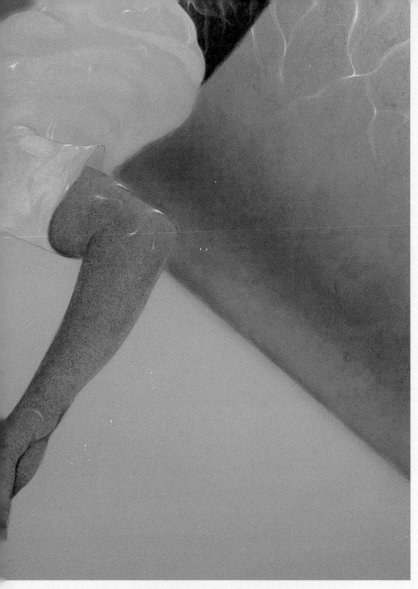

would have to get deeper yet and still have time to search while he was down there.

Stupid, he thought once more, cursing himself—just dumb. He pulled air again and again, pushing his chest out until he could not possibly get any more capacity, then took one more deep lungful, wheeled and dove again.

This time he made an arrow out of his arms and used his legs to push off the bottom of the raft, all he had in his legs, to spring-snap and propel him down. As soon as he felt himself slowing a bit he started raking back with his arms at his sides, like paddles, and thrusting with his legs like a frog and this time he was so successful that he ran his face into the bottom mud.

He shook his head to clear his eyes and looked around. The plane disappeared out and down in front of him. He thought he could see the windows and that made him think again of the pilot sitting inside and he forced his thoughts from it— but he could see no hatchet.

and he could not see bottom yet. He clawed down six or seven more feet, the pressure pushing in his ears until he held his nose and popped them and just as he ran out of breath and headed back up he thought he saw the bottom—still four feet below his dive.

He exploded out of the surface, bumping his head on the side of the elevator when he came up and took air like a whale, pushing the stale air out until he wheezed, taking new in. He

Bad air triggers were starting to go off in his brain and he knew he was limited to seconds now but he held for a moment and tried moving out a bit and just as he ran out of air, knew that he was going to have to blow soon, he saw the handle sticking out of the mud. He made one grab, missed, reached again and felt his fingers close on the rubber. He clutched it and in one motion slammed his feet down into the mud and powered himself up. But now his lungs were ready to explode and he had flashes of color in his brain, explosions of color, and he would have to take a pull of water, take it into his lungs and just as he opened his mouth to take it in, to pull in all the water in the lake his head blew out of the surface and into the light.

"Tchaaak!" It was as if a balloon had exploded. Old air blew out of his nose and mouth and he pulled new in again and again. He reached for the side of the raft and hung there, just breathing, until he could think once more—the hatchet clutched and shining in his right hand.

"All right. . . the plane. Still the plane. . ."

He went back to the hole in the fuselage and began to chop and cut again, peeling the aluminum skin off in pieces. It was slow going because he was careful, very careful with the hatchet, but he hacked and pulled until he had opened a hole large enough to pull his head and shoulders in and look down into the water. It was very dark inside the fuselage and he could see nothing—certainly no sign of the survival pack. There were some small pieces and bits of paper floating on the surface inside the plane—dirt from the floor of the plane that had floated up—but nothing substantial.

Well, he thought. Did you expect it to be easy? So easy that way? Just open her up and get the pack—right?

He would have to open it more, much more so he could poke down inside and see what he could find. The survival pack had been a zippered nylon bag, or perhaps canvas of some kind, and he thought it had been red, or was it gray?

Well, that didn't matter. It must have been moved when the plane crashed and it might be jammed down under something else.

He started chopping again, cutting the aluminum away in small triangles, putting each one on the raft as he chopped—he could never throw anything away again, he thought—because they might be useful later. Bits of metal, fish arrowheads or lures, maybe. And when he finally finished again he had cleaned away the whole side and top of the fuselage that stuck out of the water, had cut down into the water as far as he could reach and had a hole almost as big as he was, except that it was crossed and crisscrossed with aluminum—or it might be steel, he couldn't tell—braces and formers and cables. It was an awful tangled mess, but after chopping some braces away there was room for him to wiggle through and get inside.

He held back for a moment, uncomfortable with the thought of getting inside the plane. What if the tail settled back to the bottom

and he got caught and couldn't get out? It was a horrible thought. But then he reconsidered. The thing had been up now for two days, plus a bit, and he had been hammering and climbing on it and it hadn't gone back down. It seemed pretty solid.

He eeled in through the cables and formers, wiggling and pulling until he was inside the tail with his head clear of the surface of the water and his legs down on the angled floor.

plane, he thought he felt his foot hit cloth or canvas.

Up for more air, deep breathing, then one more grab at the formers and pushing as hard as he could he jammed his feet down and he hit it again, definitely canvas or heavy nylon, and this time when he pushed his foot he thought he felt something inside it; something hard.

It had to be the bag. Driven forward by the crash, it was jammed into the backs of the seats and caught on something. He tried to reach for it and pull but didn't have the air left and went up for more.

When he was ready, he took a deep breath and pushed down along the floor with his legs, feeling for some kind of fabric or cloth—anything—with his bare feet. He touched nothing but the floor plates.

Up, a new breath, then he reached down to formers underwater and pulled himself beneath the water, his legs pushing down and down almost to the backs of the front seats and finally, on the left side of the

Lungs filled in great gulps, he shot down again, pulling on the formers until he was almost there, then wheeling down head first he grabbed at the cloth. It was the survival bag. He pulled and tore at it to loosen it and just as it broke free and his heart leaped to feel it rise he looked up, above the bag. In the light coming through the side window, the pale green light from the water, he saw the pilot's head only it wasn't the pilot's head any longer.

The fish. He'd never really thought of it, but the fish—the fish he had been eating all this time had to eat, too. They had been at the pilot all this time, almost two months, nibbling and chewing and all that remained was the not quite cleaned skull and when he looked up it wobbled loosely.

Too much. Too much. His mind screamed in horror and he slammed back and was sick in the water, sick so that he choked on it and tried to breathe water and could have ended there, ended with the pilot where it almost ended when they first arrived except that his legs jerked. It was instinctive, fear more than anything else, fear of what he had seen. But they jerked and pushed and he was headed up when they jerked and he shot to the surface, still inside the birdcage of formers and cables.

His head slammed into a bracket as he cleared and he reached up to grab it and was free, in the air, hanging up in the tail.

He hung that way for several minutes, choking and heaving and gasping for air, fighting to clear

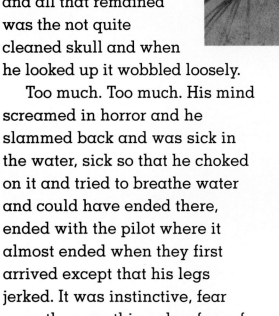

the picture of the pilot from his mind. It went slowly—he knew it would never completely leave—but he looked to the shore and there were trees and birds, the sun was getting low and golden over his shelter and when he stopped coughing he could hear the gentle sounds of evening, the peace sounds, the bird sounds and the breeze in the trees.

The peace finally came to him and he settled his breathing. He was still a long way from being finished—had a lot of work to do. The bag was floating next to him but he had to get it out of the plane and onto the raft, then back to shore.

He wiggled out through the formers—it seemed harder than when he came in—and pulled the raft around. The bag fought him. It was almost as if it didn't want to leave the plane. He pulled and jerked and still it wouldn't fit and at last he had to change the shape of it, rearranging what was inside by pushing and pulling at the sides until he had narrowed it and made it longer. Even when it finally came it was difficult and he had to pull first at one side, then another, an inch at a time, squeezing it through.

All of this took some time and when he finally got the bag out and tied on top of the raft it was nearly dark, he was bone tired from working in the water all day, chilled deep, and he still had to push the raft to shore.

Many times he thought he would not make it. With the added weight of the bag—which seemed to get heavier by the foot—coupled with the fact that he was getting weaker all the time, the raft seemed barely to move. He kicked and pulled and pushed, taking the shortest way straight back to shore, hanging to rest many times, then surging again and again.

It seemed to take forever and when at last his feet hit bottom and he could push against the mud and slide the raft into the shore weeds to bump against the bank he was so weak he couldn't stand, had to crawl; so tired he didn't even notice the mosquitoes that tore into him like a gray, angry cloud.

He had done it.

That's all he could think now. He had done it.

He turned and sat on the bank with his legs in the water and pulled the bag ashore and began the long drag—he couldn't lift it— back down the shoreline to his shelter. Two hours, almost three he dragged and stumbled in the dark, brushing the mosquitoes away, sometimes on his feet, more often on his knees, finally to drop across the bag and to sleep when he made the sand in front of the doorway.

He had done it.

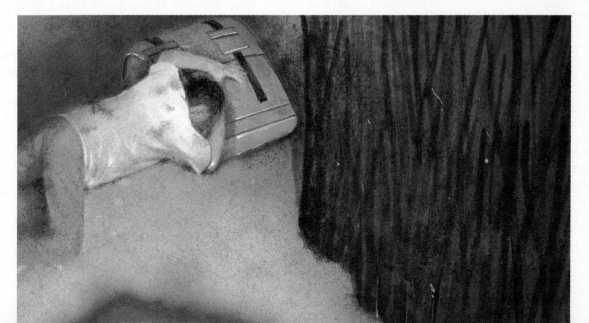

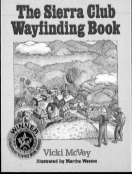

F R O M

The Sierra Club Wayfinding Book

What is a "way"? If you don't know where you are, it is something you have lost. If you don't know where you are going, it is something you are looking for. And if you do know, it is something you can show someone else. One of the most ancient skills that we possess is the ability to find our way from one place to another: *wayfinding*.

People who have been lost once don't want it to happen again, so they learn how to keep track of where they are. They do things like counting stars, marking trees, memorizing turnings, and drawing maps. But no matter what people do to keep from getting lost, all of their methods have one thing in common: they have been used before. It has been many thousands of years since we humans learned how to move around in our environment. Our primitive ancestors devised ways of figuring out where they were and how to get where they wanted to go, and we have been using and improving on their methods ever since.

By Vicki McVey

Illustrated by Karen Minot

Counting stars, drawing a map, and using a compass can help you keep track of where you are.

Gathering Information for Wayfinding

THE TASK OF MOVING around in our world, of getting from one place to another, is so automatic that we rarely even think about it. We go to school, to the store, or to a friend's house. We walk, take a bus, ride a bike, or go in a car. But getting around, like any other task, is easy only because we already know how to do it. What does that mean, to know how to do something? To begin with, it means having information.

Imagine a machine. It moves over the face of the earth gathering information. Its entire surface is covered with tiny sensors for detecting changes in the temperature, humidity, and movement of the air around it, and for sensing vibrations in the earth underneath. At the end of its two upper extendors are small probes that are so sensitive they can trace a groove one twenty-five-hundredth of an inch deep in a smooth pane of glass and can grasp and manipulate tiny objects with wonderful precision.

Near the top of the machine are two dish-shaped devices for picking up sound waves and for sensing gravity and motion. There is also a complex mechanism that emits vibrations coded as language. Inside this mechanism is a system of receptors that can detect the presence of minerals, sugars, and acids, and just above it another device for sensing odors. Its most delicate sensing devices are for receiving light waves and translating them into clear, three-dimensional, moving colored images.

The information picked up by these various sensors is sent to the storage and processing unit of the machine. This unit processes the data sent into it and issues commands according to the new information it receives. In this way it is self-regulating. It can correct its own mistakes, analyze its environment, and move purposefully from one place to another, picking up new information along the way.

Have you guessed what kind of a machine this is? Would you like to have one? If you would, I've got good news for you. You're it! You are an amazing and wonderful organism that constantly gathers and processes information about the world around you.

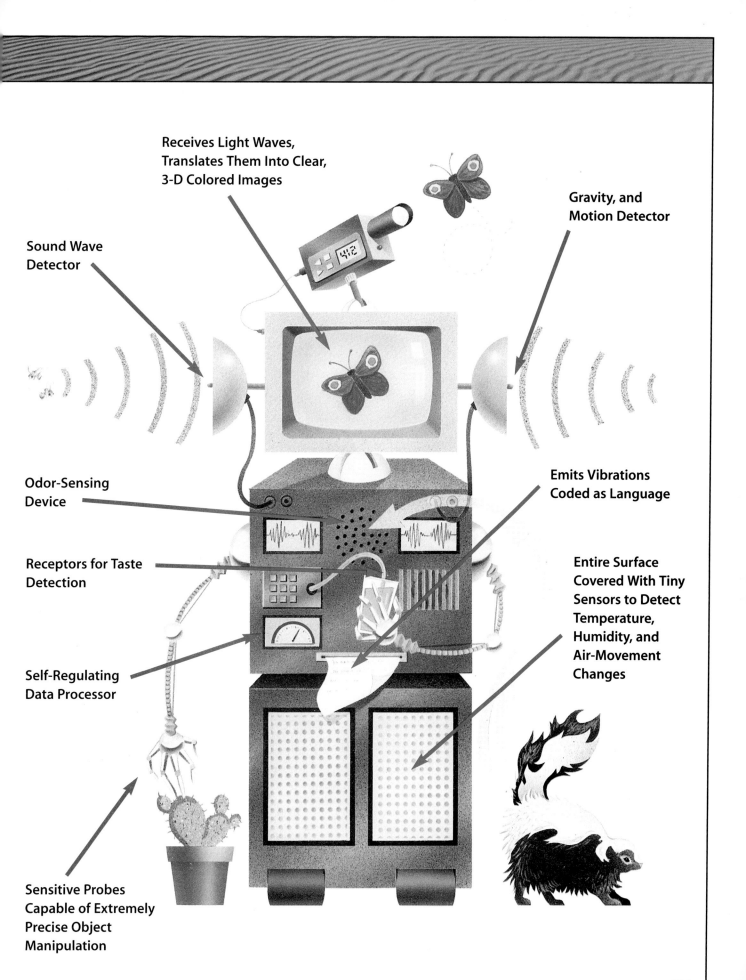

Receives Light Waves, Translates Them Into Clear, 3-D Colored Images

Sound Wave Detector

Gravity, and Motion Detector

Odor-Sensing Device

Emits Vibrations Coded as Language

Receptors for Taste Detection

Entire Surface Covered With Tiny Sensors to Detect Temperature, Humidity, and Air-Movement Changes

Self-Regulating Data Processor

Sensitive Probes Capable of Extremely Precise Object Manipulation

You use your senses of sight, hearing, touch, smell, and taste to collect information about your environment, and then you use your brain to understand the information and to make predictions and decisions. Becoming a skilled wayfinder means learning how to pay attention to and make use of all of your senses.

No other living creature "senses" the world the way we do. The bullfighter's bright red cape, waved to tantalize and enrage the charging bull, really tantalizes only the people in the audience. As far as the bull is concerned, the cape might as well be gray. In fact, to the bull and most other animals, it *is* gray, and so is everything else.

Humans are among the few creatures able to see in color. We also see in greater detail and in more depth than most other animals. And we see the world as a collection of separate objects, rather than just as a series of patterns, which is how most other animals see it.

Our sense of touch, too, is very special. Not only do we have hands like the finest of precision tools, but the nerves that give us "tactile" information are concentrated in our hands so that we can touch and feel the things we are handling. Only people and some monkeys and apes can do that.

Pigs feel with their snouts and mice feel with their whiskers, but pigs and mice can't pick things up with their noses or their whiskers. They can't hold something up to their eyes for a better view while they touch it to find out what it "feels" like. In fact, because their eyes are so close to their noses or whiskers, they can't both feel and focus their eyes on an object at the same time.

Most animals have an advantage over us humans when it comes to smelling, though. Dogs can smell at least a hundred times better than we can, and if you watch a dog you will see that it investigates the world with its nose.

Animals who get all their food by hunting often depend on their noses to help them find it. On the other hand, animals that *are* food depend on their noses to help keep them safe from the animals that are hunting *them*. A rabbit "sniffs out danger," and inside its tiny nose it has one hundred million chemoreceptor cells to help it identify odors. We haven't depended on our noses like that for millions of years.

The same thing that happened to our noses happened to our ears. As we (or our primitive human ancestors) began to find more and more of our food growing on trees or in the ground, and we didn't have to follow it as it tried to creep away from us, our ears became less important to our survival. That doesn't mean we don't use our ears. Our hearing, like our vision, is of the utmost importance in way-finding. Sound, like light, moves in waves that travel in straight lines, so our ears can help us find directions.

Our sense of taste is closely related to our sense of smell, as you may have noticed if you ever had a cold on Thanksgiving and couldn't taste the feast. Although it keeps us away from some poisons and attracts us to sugars, salts, and other nutrients, our sense of taste seems less important for survival than any of the other senses. It is also less useful in wayfinding.

When we put together the information that is gathered by all of our senses, we experience the world around us as only human beings can. Dogs live in a fuzzy black-and-white world that is full of odors and sounds we can't even detect. Many birds see one scene out of one eye and an entirely different scene out of the other. Rattlesnakes can "see" things according to how much heat they radiate, so at night these snakes move in a world full of glowing objects.

Soundwaves travel in straight lines, so our ears can help us find directions.

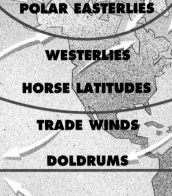

POLAR HIGH

POLAR EASTERLIES

WESTERLIES

HORSE LATITUDES

TRADE WINDS

DOLDRUMS

TRADE WINDS

HORSE LATITUDES

WESTERLIES

POLAR EASTERLIES

POLAR HIGH

Prevailing winds result from the circulation of air around the earth. The winds form six belts around the earth. The *trade winds* and *polar easterlies* flow toward the equator. The *prevailing westerlies* flow toward the poles. The *doldrums* is the region where the air heats up and rises and the *horse latitudes* is where the air cools and sinks.

Trees found in certain regions of South America are dramatically bent from the prevailing wind.

All animals, including humans, have developed their own special skills to help them survive in this world. These skills involve putting information to the best possible use. If we learn how to pay attention, how to notice the messages that our five senses are constantly sending us, not only can we find our way from place to place without being afraid of getting lost, but we will enjoy our journeys even more.

Now we know that in order to be wayfinders, *we* have to pay attention to our *environment*. There are two parts to that: the *we* part and the *environment* part. We have been talking about how *we* gather information. Now let's find out about the *environment:* clues in nature that help us know where we are.

THE WIND, for instance, brings clues to all our senses. This is especially true, whether we are in the city or the country, when we know the direction of the *prevailing wind.* Just about anywhere on earth the wind usually blows from the same direction, and this wind provides us with many clues to its presence—for example, trees with more branches on one side than on the other, and patterns in the snow or the sand.

Birds and animals naturally build their nests in the most protected places, so the presence of more nests on one side of rocks, bushes, and trees than on the other is a clue about the direction of the wind. If you see these things and already know where the prevailing wind comes from, then you automatically know which direction is which.

A bird will naturally find shelter in the most protected place on a tree.

Birds build their nests on the side of a bush that is the most protected from the wind.

The wind certainly tells our sense of touch something. You'll find that you can use the feeling of the wind on your body to maintain a constant direction when you are walking blind. And how about smell? The smell of a wind blowing off the ocean can lead you to the shore. The smell of wood smoke on the wind in the wilderness can lead you to other people.

Does the wind provide clues for our ears? Have you ever heard sounds carried on the wind? We often use sounds for locating directions, and the wind can help us do that. And finally, there's taste. Taste carried on the wind? That's not as silly as it sounds. A friend told me about being lost in a blizzard in the Arctic, and using the taste of the salt on the wind to guide him to the shore.

THE SKY is another source of natural wayfinding clues, but most sky clues are visual. Both the sun and the moon appear to travel from east to west, and can show us the cardinal directions. The stars have been our guides since people first started exploring our planet. The Caroline Islanders, some of the most famous navigators of all time, use star maps to travel throughout the islands of the Pacific Ocean.

Another natural clue in the sky is the path, or *flyway,* of migrating birds. The ancient Polynesians traveled thousands of miles from island to island using flyways to guide them. They also used clouds.

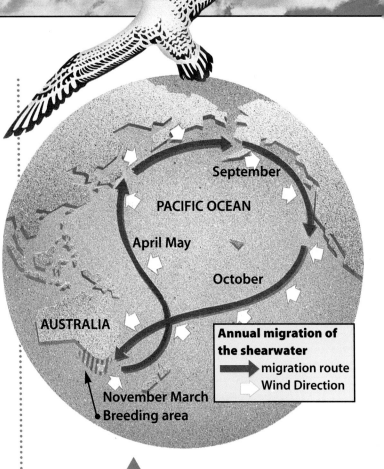

September

PACIFIC OCEAN

April May

October

AUSTRALIA

November March
Breeding area

Annual migration of the shearwater
→ migration route
⇨ Wind Direction

The short-tailed shearwater breeds around southeastern Australia, then circles almost the entire Pacific Ocean before returning for the next breeding season.

◀ A star map

In the Arctic and on the ocean, the underside of clouds acts like a mirror and reflects the presence of open water in the middle of ice, an iceberg in the ocean, or an island in the open ocean. An oasis in the desert is indicated from far away by the special haze it creates in the air above it.

Most of us are more likely to use the natural clues provided by various plants. In hilly areas, trees and bushes that grow on slopes facing north are different from those that grow on slopes facing south, and this difference in vegetation can tell you in which direction you're walking. Many plants orient themselves toward the sun, like the old man of the mountain, whose flowers face east. Other plants, like the compass plant, align their leaves in a north-south direction to provide themselves with shade. As with the prevailing wind, you have to get to know an area to learn how to read these natural clues.

Compass Plant
leaves align north–south

Old Man of the Mountain
flowers face east

THE ENVIRONMENT provides us with information, our senses collect that information and send it to our brains, but what do our brains do with it? In the case of wayfinding, we store the information in "mental recordings" of the environment. Then, when necessary, we extract the appropriate bits of information and put them together as "mental maps." We are not even aware of this process.

Stop for a minute and think about how you get to your best friend's house, or to school. What did you do? If you're like most people you conjured up stored information: "Um . . . there's an ugly red house on the corner where I go left until I get to a noisy, busy street. That's the street before my friend's house, so I cross it, go one more block, turn right at the corner with the dog that always barks at me, and my friend's house is the third one on the left." That is a mental map. Did you notice that the "waysigns" ("ugly red house," "noisy, busy street," "corner with the dog") either indicate places to turn or confirm that the pathfinder is on the right course?

Like most mental maps, this one could be transferred to a scrap of paper and given to someone else who could then use it to get to the same place. Each person has her or his own absolutely unique mental maps, because each of us notices different things as we make our way from place to place. Of all the thousands and thousands of maps in the world, the most numerous and often used are the ones we carry around inside our heads.

Now we have a complete cycle: our five senses collect the information that the environment is presenting, and our brains process that information and make it available to us in the form of mental maps that help us get from place to place. The trick is that the more we notice, the more complete and accurate our mental maps will be.

What If You Do Get Lost?

BEFORE WE FINISH, there's one more thing I'd like to talk about. I would like to leave you with some suggestions about what to do if you should ever lose your way. We will talk about two kinds of being lost: lost in the country, and lost in the city.

First of all, the most important thing to know about being lost is that you have to keep your mind clear for thinking. In other words, *don't panic.* Even if it's a scary situation, give yourself a few minutes to calm down before you make any big moves. If you are lost in the wilderness, remember that there are people close by who are at least as anxious to find you as you are to be found, and if everyone thinks clearly and without panic, that's just what will happen. If you are lost in the city, there will be people around that you can ask for help.

When you are hiking or back-packing, there are certain things you should always carry with you. The trouble is, one of the times when people get lost in the wilderness is when they think they are going only a "short" distance away from camp (to get water, dig a latrine, or just be alone for a few minutes), and so they don't have their packs with them. Even though they might have emergency and first-aid provisions, their packs are left leaning up against a tree back at camp.

Since that is often the case, there are some things that you should always carry somewhere on your body. The most important of these is a good, loud whistle. Get one that makes lots of noise, and hang it around your neck. Remember that it is an emergency signaling device and should *never* be used except in the case of a real emergency. If you get lost or separated from the rest of your group, or if you are hurt and can't catch up with them, you can create a loud signal that can be heard for quite a distance.

The international distress signal is a series of three repeated signals of any kind. So blow three blasts on your whistle, pause for a little while, blow three more blasts, pause,

and keep repeating the signal. Once you are certain that you are lost or in need of help, stay where you are. Don't continue wandering around, because the chances are that you will wander in the wrong direction and get even further separated from your group.

Some of the other things you should always carry with you are: water (you can get the kind of bottle that hangs from your belt) and water purifying tablets, a pocket knife, matches in a plastic Baggie, and some sort of high-energy food (trail mix, a high-protein candy bar, or anything else you can think of that will fit in your pockets). These are things you can keep with you at all times, even when you don't have your pack. Another suggestion, though it may sound pretty strange, is to carry a large plastic trash bag in one of your pockets. Plastic is good insulation, besides being waterproof, and if you cut a slit in the top and two in the sides for your head and arms, you will have a ready-made body warmer.

If you become lost in the wilderness, stay calm, try to keep warm, avoid fatigue, and try to find a way of signaling your location.

It is a good idea to carry a whistle, a canteen for water, trail mix, water purifying tablets, and a large plastic bag when you go on a hike.

WATER PURIFYER

**If you're lost, you may want to build a fire as an emergency signal,
to attract the attention of search planes.**

If you are lost for more than a few hours and find yourself in a survival situation, establish a camp. The best place for this is high, clear ground, but it is better to stay where you are than to wander for miles looking for a good location. If you need to leave your camp (to look for firewood or water, for instance), mark a clear trail so you can find your way back. Don't ever try to travel at night.

When you are lost, you want to improve the situation without further endangering yourself. The last thing you want to do is make things worse, so think before you do anything. If you decide to climb a tree to get a better view, for example, choose a safe one that is easy to get up and down.

Because fires are visible for great distances, especially at night, it is possible to use them as emergency signals. Airplanes flying overhead, or any other searchers, may take note of your fire and report it or come to investigate. But fires can also be terribly dangerous. If you decide to build a fire, do it right. Choose a clear place well away from trees with low-hanging branches. Make a stone ring and dig a shallow pit in the center of it. Before you build the fire, gather as much firewood as you can and keep it well away from the blaze. You can keep the fire small by feeding it only small amounts of wood. Watch over it constantly. DO NOT LET A FIRE GET OUT OF CONTROL, AND NEVER BUILD A FIRE IN STRONG WIND.

Few of us have ever seen a raging forest fire, but anyone who has knows what it can do. You need to respect fire and have a good, healthy terror of it getting out of control. If you get lost, the chances are that you will survive; if you are in a forest fire, the chances are that you won't. It is that simple, so be careful with fire. When you are camping with your family or any other group, ask someone to teach you how to make and maintain a safe fire.

BEING LOST IN THE CITY involves a completely different set of problems. If you are lost in a city where people speak English, at least you can ask for help. But even in that case, you have to know what to ask. No matter where you are, if you are visiting a strange city, be sure to carry something with you that has your address on it. This can be especially important in countries where people don't speak English.

If you are staying in a hotel, carry a piece of hotel stationery or a book of matches that identifies the hotel and its location. Have someone write, in the language that is spoken there, something like "Please take me to" or "Where is" next to the address. Talk to your parents or the group you are traveling with, and establish a rule that if anyone gets separated, they will meet the rest of the group back at the hotel. This will save wear and tear on everyone's nerves.

It is easier to get lost in a city than you might think. I was once walking in New Delhi, India, with an American family. We were making our way down an extremely crowded street when their little girl very suddenly just disappeared. One minute she was there, and the next she was lost in the crowd. There were thousands of people on the sidewalk, and she disappeared into the masses. Fortunately, we soon found her again, but we had a frightening few moments when we thought about how impossible it would be to find anyone in that crowd of people whose language we didn't speak.

If you are lost in the city, the best person to ask for help, whether you speak the language or not, is a police officer. Don't be afraid to ask; it is his or her job to give assistance. If you can't find a uniformed police officer, go into any fairly prosperous-looking business establishment and ask one of the employees to help you. People will most likely be very interested and sympathetic, and if you are a shy person you might not like all the attention, but someone will see that you get back to the address you have written on the piece of paper.

Whether you are lost in the city or the wilderness, keep a clear head and make thoughtful decisions. Don't panic. Someone is looking for you, too, and if you're careful and smart you'll find each other. The best way to avoid the problem of needing to get found, of course, is not to get lost. Practice wayfinding as if your life depends on it, and enjoy the journeys that take you on your way.

A street map of Atlanta, Georgia

STAYING ALIVE

BY DAVID WAGONER
ILLUSTRATED BY DANUTA JARECKA

Staying alive in the woods is a matter of calming down
At first and deciding whether to wait for rescue,
Trusting to others,
Or simply to start walking and walking in one direction
Till you come out—or something happens to stop you.
By far the safer choice
Is to settle down where you are, and try to make a living
Off the land, camping near water, away from shadows.
Eat no white berries;
Spit out all bitterness. Shooting at anything
Means hiking further and further every day
To hunt survivors;
It may be best to learn what you have to learn without a gun,
Not killing but watching birds and animals go
In and out of shelter
At will. Following their example, build for a whole season:
Facing across the wind in your lean-to,
You may feel wilder,
But nothing, not even you, will have to stay in hiding.
If you have no matches, a stick and a fire-bow
Will keep you warmer,
Or the crystal of your watch, filled with water, held up to the sun
Will do the same in time. In case of snow
Drifting toward winter,
Don't try to stay awake through the night, afraid of freezing—
The bottom of your mind knows all about zero;

It will turn you over
And shake you till you waken. If you have trouble sleeping
Even in the best of weather, jumping to follow
With eyes strained to their corners
The unidentifiable noises of the night and feeling
Bears and packs of wolves nuzzling your elbow,
Remember the trappers
Who treated them indifferently and were left alone.
If you hurt yourself, no one will comfort you
Or take your temperature,
So stumbling, wading, and climbing are as dangerous as flying.
But if you decide, at last, you must break through
In spite of all danger,
Think of yourself by time and not by distance, counting
Wherever you're going by how long it takes you;
No other measure
Will bring you safe to nightfall. Follow no streams: they run
Under the ground or fall into wilder country.
Remember the stars
And moss when your mind runs into circles. If it should rain
Or the fog should roll the horizon in around you,
Hold still for hours
Or days if you must, or weeks, for seeing is believing
In the wilderness. And if you find a pathway,
Wheel, rut, or fence, wire,
Retrace it left or right: someone knew where he was going
Once upon a time, and you can follow
Hopefully, somewhere,
Just in case. There may even come, on some uncanny evening,

A time when you're warm and dry, well fed, not thirsty,
Uninjured, without fear,
When nothing, either good or bad, is happening.
This is called staying alive. It's temporary.
What occurs after
Is doubtful. You must always be ready for something to come bursting
Through the far edge of a clearing, running toward you,
Grinning from ear to ear
And hoarse with welcome. Or something crossing and hovering
Overhead, as light as air, like a break in the sky,
Wondering what you are.
Here you are face to face with the problem of recognition.
Having no time to make smoke, too much to say,
You should have a mirror
With a tiny hole in the back for better aiming, for reflecting
Whatever disaster you can think of, to show
The way you suffer.
These body signals have universal meaning: If you are lying
Flat on your back with arms outstretched behind you,
You say you require
Emergency treatment; if you are standing erect and holding
Arms horizontal, you mean you are not ready;
If you hold them over
Your head, you want to be picked up. Three of anything
Is a sign of distress. Afterward, if you see
No ropes, no ladders,
No maps or messages falling, no searchlights or trails blazing,
Then, chances are, you should be prepared to burrow
Deep for a deep winter.

How to

Write a Survival Guide

Use **atlases,** *maps,* and other **resources** to create a *survival* guide to a **new** place.

What would travelers do to prepare themselves for a challenging new environment? Would they need to pack heavy rain gear in case of a hurricane? water in case of a drought? insect repellent for pesky insects? First, they would research the place they are traveling to. Then, they might read a survival guide. A survival guide includes all the important things someone needs to know to meet the challenges and problems of a new environment.

SUPPLIES

hat
sunscree
water
food
matche
bathin
sanda
sungl

The Desert Island Survival Guide

Choose Your Site

Make a list of places for which visitors might need a survival guide. The place may be a wilderness environment, such as a rain forest or a remote mountain range. Look at maps and reference books for ideas. Talk to people. Ask them about interesting places that they have been to or heard about. Travel sections of newspapers and magazines will provide ideas, too. Be sure to pick a place that you are interested in or that you've always wanted to visit.

TOOLS

- map
- reference books
- markers
- foreign phrase books

After you've chosen your place, make a list of questions that your guide will answer. What are some of the questions you yourself have about the place you have chosen? What kinds of facts should your guide contain? Refer to your list as you do your research. You may think of more questions as you go along.

2 Get the Facts

Once you've decided on a site and thought of questions to be answered, it is time to gather your facts. Look in an atlas or an encyclopedia for information. Magazine or newspaper articles will be helpful as well. You could also visit a travel agency and pick up some travel brochures about the area.

If you can, talk to people who come from or have visited the place. As you do research, here are some questions to think about.

- What is the weather like?

- What are the plants, animals, and land regions like?

- What type of clothing do the people living there wear?

- Are there any special customs that would be important to know?

- What language do the people speak?

- What kind of money is used?

- What are the most common forms of transportation—boat, horseback, subway?

Take notes as you do your research. You may want to sketch a map of your area from an atlas.

How Am I Doing?

Before you create your survival guide, take a minute to ask yourself these questions:

- Have I gathered information about the geographical features and the plants and animals?

- Have I gathered information about languages and other customs?

Put the Pieces Together

Your survival guide will include several sections.

• **Atlas page**. This page includes facts about your place and one or more maps.

• **Equipment list**. This lists all the equipment a person would need to bring to make his or her stay comfortable and safe.

• **Cultural traditions.** This page tells visitors the customs and traditions of the place.

• **Drawings of common plants and animals**. Help visitors to identify unique or dangerous plants and animals.

• **Handy phrases**. If a foreign language is spoken, you may want to list some words and phrases that a visitor needs to know.

 Is there important information that won't fit on these pages? You may want to add an extra page called "More Survival Tips" that includes first-aid information, for example.

4 Present Your Survival Guide

Present your survival guide to your classmates. Decide on a form for your presentation. You can:

- Give your guide to people who are interested in visiting the place you've written about. Ask them what new things they learned.

- Give an oral presentation to a few of your classmates. Use the guide as a visual aid. If it's possible, you can put parts of your guide on transparencies and use an overhead projector as you give your presentation.

If You Are Using a Computer ...

Create your survival guide in the Report format on the computer. Browse through the clip art library to find pictures of animals and maps to use in your guide. Use the title page maker to create a cover for your guide.

CONGRATULATIONS

You've learned to survive in new environments. Remember—planning will help you meet new challenges successfully.

Cesar Rivera
Emergency Worker ▶

Glossary

an•chored
(ang´ kərd) *verb*
Held in place under the water. The treasure chest was *anchored* at the bottom of the sea by a large rock.
▲ **anchor**

as•cent
(ə sent´) *noun*
An upward movement. As we continued our *ascent*, the valley appeared smaller beneath us.

ascent

bid•ding
(bid´ ing) *noun*
An order or a command. We had no choice but to do the king's *bidding*.

coast
(kōst) *noun*
Land near the edge of the sea.

cre•vas•ses
(krə vas´ iz) *noun*
Deep cracks in glacial ice or in the earth's surface. The deep *crevasses* criss-crossed the mountain.
▲ **crevasse**

crude
(krōōd) *adjective*
Showing a lack of expertise; rough. She made a *crude* shelter out of branches and twigs.

drought
(drout) *noun*
A long period of little or no rainfall that can stop the growth of plants.

fierce
(fērs) *adjective*
Ferocious; hostile.

Thesaurus

fierce
wild
savage
vicious

fis•sures
(fish´ ərz) *noun*
Long, narrow cracks produced by a separation of parts. The *fissures* in the rock showed iron ore inside. ▲ **fissure**

fly•way
(flī′ wā′) *noun*
The route between summer and winter homes of migrating birds. The songbirds' *flyway* started in South America and ended in Canada.

hatch•et
(hach′ it) *noun*
A small ax with a short handle designed to be used with one hand.

I•dit•a•rod
(ī dit′ ə räd′) *noun*
An annual dogsled race along the Iditarod Trail in Alaska.

ig•loo
(ig′ lo͞o) *noun*
An Eskimo house made of snow blocks and shaped like a dome.

Word History

Igloo means "snow house" in the Eskimo language.

igloo

in•stinc•tive
(in stingk′ tiv) *adjective*
Driven by an inner or natural feeling. The dog's *instinctive* sense told it to stay clear of the rattlesnake.

king•doms
(king′ dəmz) *noun*
Governments ruled by kings or queens.
▲ **kingdom**

lev•ee
(lev′ ē) *noun*
A wall built up along a river to keep it from flooding. The river rose over its banks, but the *levee* held the water back.

men•tal maps
(men′ tl maps) *noun*
Visual images of an area committed to memory. She had *mental maps* of the routes to school and to the library. ▲ **mental map**

a	add	o͞o	took	ə =
ā	ace	o͞o	pool	a in *above*
â	care	u	up	e in *sicken*
ä	palm	û	burn	i in *possible*
e	end	yo͞o	fuse	o in *melon*
ē	equal	oi	oil	u in *circus*
i	it	ou	pout	
ī	ice	ng	ring	
o	odd	th	thin	
ō	open	th	this	
ô	order	zh	vision	

Glossary

muk·luks
(muk′ luks) *noun*
Eskimo boots made of the skin of a seal or reindeer.
▲ **mukluk**

Word History

Mukluk comes from the Eskimo word *muklok,* which means "large seal."

mush·ers
(mush′ ərz) *noun*
Dogsled drivers.
▲ **musher**

nav·i·ga·tors
(nav′ i gā tərz) *noun*
People who set or direct the course of a ship, airplane, or spacecraft.
▲ **navigator**

op·er·at·ing base
(op′ ə rāt ing bās) *noun*
A location where useful work is performed.

out·dis·tance
(out′ dis′ təns) *verb*
To travel farther than or way ahead of someone or something else. He knew he had to *outdistance* the runner before the end of the race.

over·come
(ō′ vər kum′) *verb*
To rise above difficulties.

path·find·er
(path′ fin dər) *noun*
A person who discovers a new way through an unknown area.

por·ters
(pôr′ tərz) *noun*
People hired to carry things, especially baggage.
▲ **porter**

prec·i·pice
(pres′ ə pis) *noun*
A very steep or overhanging mass of rock, similar to a cliff. We looked very carefully over the edge of the *precipice.*

pre·vail·ing wind
(pri vā′ ling wind) *noun*
The most common direction of the wind.

riv·er sys·tem
(riv′ ər sis′ təm) *noun*
A river and the smaller rivers and streams that flow into it.

run·ners
(run′ ərz) *noun*
The long, narrow metal or wood strips on which a sled slides. We were forced to stop when our *runners* got stuck in the ice.
▲ **runner**

sand·bag·gers
(sand′ bag ərz) *noun*
People who use bags filled with sand to build a protective wall.
▲ **sandbagger**

star map
(stär map) *noun*
A representation or drawing of the groups of stars in the night sky. Early sailors used *star maps* to help them steer their ships.

Fact File

People have been creating star maps for thousands of years. The oldest star map was painted in 25 B.C. It was discovered in 1987 on the ceiling of a tomb in Xian, China.

sty·mied
(stī′ mēd) *verb*
Faced with a block or obstacle. I was *stymied* by the cow in the middle of the road. ▲ **stymie**

sum·mit
(sum′ it) *noun*
The highest point.

Thesaurus

summit

apex
peak
top

tid·al wave
(tīd´ l wāv) *noun*
An unusually large
destructive wave caused
by an earthquake, volcano,
storm, or a combination
of wind and tide.

Fact File

Tidal waves caused by
earthquakes or volcanoes
can be up to 200 miles long
and move at speeds up to
500 miles per hour, growing
to a height of 100 feet
upon reaching the shore.

tow·line
(tō´ līn) *noun*
A rope or chain used by a
vehicle or animal to pull
something else.

tri·an·gu·la·tion
(trī ang´ gyə lā´ shən)
noun
A way of measuring height
or distance based on
trigonometry, the study of
triangles.

trib·u·tar·ies
(trib´ yə ter´ ēz) *noun*
Streams that flow into a
larger river or stream.
▲ **tributary**

tributaries

ven·ture
(ven´ chər) *noun*
To go forward in spite of
risk or danger ahead.

wad·ers
(wā´ dərz) *noun*
High, waterproof boots.
▲ **wader**

waders

way·find·ing
(wā fīnd´ ing) *noun*
The art of finding the way
from one place to another
using valuable clues. We
practiced *wayfinding* in the
woods behind our house.

way·signs
(wā´ sīnz) *noun*
Clues used to help a
person find the way from
one place to another.
These could include
landmarks, maps, and the
position of the sun.
▲ **waysign**

wind·break·er
(wind´ brā´ kər) *noun*
A type of jacket made of
material that helps protect
the body from wind.

a	add	o͝o	took	ə =
ā	ace	o͞o	pool	a in *above*
â	care	u	up	e in *sicken*
ä	palm	û	burn	i in *possible*
e	end	yo͞o	fuse	o in *melon*
ē	equal	oi	oil	u in *circus*
i	it	ou	pout	
ī	ice	ng	ring	
o	odd	th	thin	
ō	open	th	this	
ô	order	zh	vision	

Authors & Illustrators

Ashley Bryan   *pages 10–19*

Ashley Bryan has received the Coretta Scott King Award and other recognition for his illustrations, but he feels his greatest satisfaction comes from the response of people he knows. He bases his illustrations on the African art he has studied in museums and libraries. After working as a professor of art at Dartmouth College for many years, he now lives, paints, and writes on an island in Maine.

Walter Dean Myers   *pages 10–19*

Books have always been important to Walter Dean Myers. While growing up in Harlem, New York, he read avidly, making the local public library his "most treasured place." He writes his popular and much-praised books about problems that bother him, as a way of "looking for the answers."

Scott O'Dell   *pages 68–81*

This Newbery Medal-winning author is remembered for his action-packed historical novels. Born in 1898, O'Dell's early memories of adventures in the hills around his home inspired the settings and drama of his books. He also did months of research to give each of his novels authentic details. He wrote right up to his death in 1989.

Gary Paulsen *pages 92–107*

Like the characters in his books, this author is no stranger to the outdoors. Before Paulsen became an award-winning author, he worked as a farmer, rancher, trapper, and sailor. He even raced sled dogs in the Alaskan Iditarod race. Paulsen also loves the challenge of writing; he has written over 40 books and 200 magazine articles. He continues to write at his home in Wyoming.

"When I find a story, my breath quickens, my hair goes up on my neck—the story is what makes writing books so incredibly fine."

Doreen Rappaport *pages 42–59*

Doreen Rappaport collected the first-person stories in *American Women: Their Lives in Their Words*, as well as writing about these women in *Living Dangerously*. She has also written several other books about the contributions women have made throughout history. She continues to explore these subjects in her books.

Henri Rousseau *pages 20–21*

A self-taught painter, Rousseau worked as a government clerk and could not paint full-time until he retired. In his time he was criticized for not painting in a familiar style, though many of the young artists of Paris admired him. He died in 1910, and his colorful and imaginative compositions are even more respected today.

Books &

Author Study

More by Scott O'Dell

Black Pearl
In this gripping story, Ramon learns the family art of pearl diving and respect for the legend of the giant pearl he finds.

Carlotta
A young girl relates her feelings and experiences in the final days of the Mexican War.

Zia
A Native American girl handles the pull of two different worlds with the help of her aunt, Karana, the heroine of *The Island of the Blue Dolphins*.

Fiction

The River
by Gary Paulsen
Brian has a wounded partner and a long river to navigate if they are to survive in this exciting sequel to *Hatchet*.

Julie of the Wolves
by Jean Craighead George
In order to get through the harsh Arctic winter, Julie, a resourceful Inuit girl, lives and hunts with a pack of wolves.

The Story of Lightning & Thunder
by Ashley Bryan
In this funny African folk tale about the power of nature, Lightning is a young ram who finds out that butting his way out of trouble is not the best approach.

Nonfiction

The True Adventures of Grizzly Adams
by Robert McClung
This biography describes the life of the mountain man who got his nickname from his close association with bears.

Volcanoes and Earthquakes
by Mary Elting
Throughout history, people have had to cope with natural disasters. This book tells the story of major earthquakes and volcanoes and how people rebuilt after them.

Wilderness Challenge
compiled by the editors of National Geographic
This beautifully photographed book highlights the skills it takes to survive in the wilderness.

Media

Videos

The Black Stallion
Disney
This movie adaptation of Walter Farley's classic novel involves a boy and a horse who are shipwrecked on a deserted island. (118 minutes)

Search for the Great Apes
National Geographic Video
(Vestron/FHE)
Join Dian Fossey as she researches how mountain gorillas survive in the wild, and see how another scientist, Birute Galdikas Brindamour, introduces a baby orangutan born in captivity to the rain forest in Borneo. (60 minutes)

The Story of 15 Boys
Celebrity/Just for Kids
Shipwrecked students from an English school must pull together in order to survive. This exciting animated film is based on the novel *Two Years Vacation* by Jules Verne. (80 minutes)

Software

The Lost Tribe
Lawrence
(Apple II, Macintosh, IBM)
This leadership strategy game is set in prehistoric times and includes photos, video clips, sound effects, and an on-screen "Prehistoric Guide to Survival."

Puddles to Pondwater
Niad Corporation
(IBM)
Join the World Biological Council in its quest to save the earth's wildlife from environmental emergencies.

Swiss Family Robinson
Orange Cherry
(Macintosh-CD-ROM)
Only you can help the Swiss Family Robinson survive in their desert island habitat. This simulation is based on the classic novel.

Magazines

National Geographic World
National Geographic Society
This publication features articles about outdoor adventures as well as information about science, history, and other topics.

Owl Magazine
Young Naturalist Foundation
Each issue of this Canadian magazine offers information, games, and puzzles about habitats, technology, animals, and more.

A Place to Write

If you live in a city, you may seldom get to see an actual forest or mountains. Inner City Outings can send you on a wilderness adventure in the city. Write to them for information.

Inner City Outings
Sierra Club
730 Polk St.
San Francisco, CA 94109

Acknowledgments

Grateful acknowledgment is made to the following sources for permission to reprint from previously published material. The publisher has made diligent efforts to trace the ownership of all copyrighted material in this volume and believes that all necessary permissions have been secured. If any errors or omissions have inadvertently been made, proper corrections will gladly be made in future editions.

Cover: CH 21094 THE GREAT WAVE OF KANAGAWA, from the series "36 Views of Mt. Fuji" ("Fugaku sanjuokkei") published by Nishimura Eijudo, 1831, (color woodblock print) by Katsushika Hokusai (1760-1849) Christie's, London/Bridgeman Art Library.

Interior: "The Story of the Three Kingdoms" from THE STORY OF THE THREE KINGDOMS by Walter Dean Myers, illustrated by Ashley Bryan. Text copyright © 1995 by Walter Dean Myers. Illustrations copyright © 1995 by Ashley Bryan. Reprinted by permission of HarperCollins Publishers.

"The Sleeping Gypsy" and cover from HENRI ROUSSEAU by Ernest Raboff from ART FOR CHILDREN series. Published by HarperCollins Publishers. First Harper Trophy edition, 1988.

"Along the Levee as People Fight a Tireless River" by Sara Rimer from The New York Times, July 14, 1993. Text copyright © 1993 by The New York Times Company. Reprinted by permission.

"Tales of Valor, Fear, and Kindness" from The Kansas City Star, July 10, 1993. Text copyright © 1993 by The Kansas City Star. Reprinted by permission.

"Teens Find It's Fun to Make a Difference" from The Des Moines Register, July 26, 1993. Text copyright © 1993 by The Des Moines Register and Tribune Company. Reprinted by permission.

"What are you fishing for?..." cartoon from San Diego Union-Tribune, July 26, 1993. Copyright © 1993 by Steve Kelley—San Diego Union-Tribune. Reprinted by permission of Copley News Service.

North Africa atlas page on page 37 is an excerpt from THE CHILDREN'S ATLAS OF PEOPLE AND PLACES by Jenny Wood and David Munro. Copyright © 1993 by Quarto Publishing plc. Reprinted by permission of the publisher.

"The Mountain That Refused to Be Climbed" and cover from LIVING DANGEROUSLY: AMERICAN WOMEN WHO RISKED THEIR LIVES FOR ADVENTURE by Doreen Rappaport. Copyright © 1991 by Doreen Rappaport. Reprinted by permission of HarperCollins Publishers.

Selection and cover from SCHOLASTIC ATLAS OF EXPLORATION by Dinah Starkey. Text and illustrations copyright © 1993 by HarperCollins Publishers Ltd. Reprinted by permission of HarperCollins Publishers Ltd.

Selection and cover from BLACK STAR, BRIGHT DAWN by Scott O'Dell. Text copyright © 1988 by Scott O'Dell. Reprinted by permission of Houghton Mifflin Company. All rights reserved.

"The Last Great Race" from Action magazine, April 3, 1987. Copyright © 1987 by Scholastic Inc. Reprinted by permission.

"Equipment Checklist" used by the kind permission of Above the Clouds Trekking, Worchester, MA.

Selection from HATCHET by Gary Paulsen. Text copyright © 1987 by Gary Paulsen. Reprinted by arrangement with Simon & Schuster Books for Young Readers, Simon & Schuster Children's Publishing Division. Cover illustration by Neil Waldman. Copyright © by Neil Waldman. Reprinted by permission of the illustrator.

Selections and cover from THE SIERRA CLUB WAYFINDING BOOK by Vicki McVey. Text copyright © 1989 by Vicki McVey. Cover illustration copyright © 1989 by Martha Weston. Reprinted by permission of Little, Brown and Company.

"Staying Alive" by David Wagoner from NEW AND SELECTED POEMS BY DAVID WAGONER. Copyright © by David Wagoner. Reprinted by permission of the author.

Cover from THE BIG WAVE by Pearl S. Buck, illustrated by Wendell Minor. Illustration copyright © 1986 by Wendell Minor. Published by HarperCollins Children's Books, a division of HarperCollins Publishers.

Cover from ISLAND OF THE BLUE DOLPHINS by Scott O'Dell, illustrated by Keith Batcheller. Copyright © 1987 by Keith Batcheller. Published by Dell Publishing, a division of Bantam Doubleday Dell Publishing Group, Inc.

Cover from MY SIDE OF THE MOUNTAIN by Jean Craighead George, illustrated by Michael Garland. Illustration copyright © 1989 by Michael Garland. Published by Viking Penguin, a division of Penguin Books USA Inc.

Cover from THE OSTRICH CHASE by Moses L. Howard, illustrated by Beatrice Lebreton. Illustration copyright © 1995 by Scholastic Inc. Published by Scholastic Inc.

Photography and Illustration Credits

Photos: All Tools in Workshops and Project © John Lei for Scholastic Inc. unless otherwise noted. p. 2 bl, ml, tl: © John Lei for Scholastic Inc. pp. 2-3 c: © Paul S. Howell for Scholastic Inc. p. 3 bc: © Paul S. Howell for Scholastic Inc.; tc: © Arnuf Husmo/Tony Stone Worldwide. p. 4 c: © Rich Miller for Scholastic Inc.; tc: © Arnuf Husmo/Tony Stone Worldwide. p. 5 c: © Francis Clark Westfield for Scholastic Inc.; tc: © Arnuf Husmo/Tony Stone Worldwide. p. 6 c: © Ana Esperanza Nance for Scholastic Inc.; tc: © Arnuf Husmo/Tony Stone Worldwide. p. 21: © The Sleeping Gypsy by Henri Rousseau, Museum of Modern Art, gift of Mrs. Simon Guggenheim. pp. 22-23 c: © B. Gillette/Gamma Liaison. p. 24 bc: © Monica Almeida/NYT Pictures. p. 25 tr: © Jeff Beierman/AP Wide World. p. 28 bl: © Jym Wilson/Gannett News Service; bl: © Paul S. Howell for Scholastic Inc.; c: © Arnuf Husmo/Tony Stone Worldwide; ml: © Paul S. Howell for Scholastic Inc.; tl: © Paul S. Howell for Scholastic Inc.; tr: © D.A.R.T. p. 29 c: © B. Neibergall/Des Moines Register. p. 30 tl: © John Gaps III/AP Wide World. p. 31 bl: © Les Stone/Sygma; br: © S. Kelly/San Diego Union Tribune; tc: © Christiansen/Gamma Liaison. pp. 32-33 bc: © John Lei for Scholastic Inc. p. 33 br: © John Lei for Scholastic Inc; tr: © John Lei for Scholastic Inc. p. 35 certificates: © John Lei for Scholastic Inc. p. 38 c: © Stanley Bach for Scholastic Inc. pp. 38-39 bc: © John Lei for Scholastic Inc. p. 39 br: © John Lei for Scholastic Inc. p. 42 c: © Brown Bros. p. 44 bc: © Mary Altier/The Travel Image. p. 45 br: © Brian Yarvia/Photo Researchers, Inc.; tr: © Charlie Benes/Photo Bank. p. 46 mr: © Rhode Island Historical Society; tl: © The Granger Collection, NY. p. 48 tl: © Archive Photos. p. 49 bl: © The Granger Collection, NY; tr: © Mario Corvetto/Comstock Inc. p. 50 tr: © Georgia Engelhard/FPG International Corp. p. 51 bl: © Brown Bros.; tc: © The Granger Collection, NY. p. 52 bl: © The Granger Collection, NY. pp. 53-57 tc: © Courtesy National Geographic Society. p. 61 br: HUMBOLDT IN HIS LIBRARY, © Royal Geographical Society, London/Bridgeman Art Library. p. 58 tc: © G.M. Doyette/The National Geographic Society. p. 59 bc: © All Rights Reserved, The Rhode Island Historical Society. p. 62 bl: © The Mary Evans Picture Library. p. 63 mr: WILLIAM BARENT'S HUT IN NOVAYA ZEMBYA, © 1957 British Library, London/Bridgeman Art Library. p. 64 ml: © Mary Evans Picture Library. p. 66 ml: © David Baughan/SPL/Photo Researchers. pp. 66-67 c: © Photo Library International Inc. p. 67 br: © NASA/SPL/Photo Researchers. pp. 82-83 c: © Chris Arend/Alaska Stock. p. 84 ml: © Anchorage Daily News/Gamma Liaison; tl: © Jeff Schultz/Alaska Stock. pp. 84-85 background: © Jeff Schultz/Alaska Stock. p. 85 tc: © Jeff Schultz/Sygma. p. 86 br, mr: © David Lawrence for Scholastic Inc. pp. 86-87 background: © Charles Krebs/The Stock Market. p. 87 br: © Richard Megna for Scholastic Inc. pp. 88-89 bc: © Stanley Bach for Scholastic Inc. p. 89 br: © John Lei for Scholastic Inc. pp. 108 bl: © Stanley Bach for Scholastic Inc.; ml: © Ken Karp for Scholastic Inc. pp. 108-109 tc: © Telegraph